P9-BBU-864

PRESENTED TO:

_____

FROM:

_____

DATE:

_____

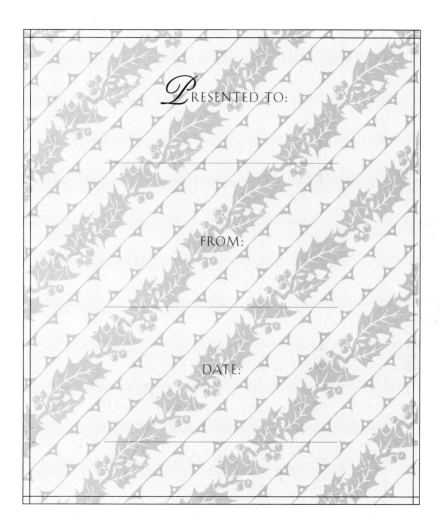

$\mathcal{P}$RESENTED TO:

_____

FROM:

_____

DATE:

_____

CHRISTMAS
ABUNDANCE

A SIMPLE GUIDE TO
DISCOVERING THE TRUE
MEANING OF CHRISTMAS

CANDY PAULL

OLIVER
NELSON ™

THOMAS NELSON PUBLISHERS
Nashville

Published in Nashville, Tennessee, by Thomas Nelson, Inc.

Scripture quotations noted RSV are from the REVISED STANDARD VERSION of the Bible. Copyright © 1946, 1952, 1971, 1973 by the Division of Christian Education of the National Council of the Churches of Christ in the U.S.A. Used by permission.

Scripture quotations noted KJV are from the Holy Bible, KING JAMES VERSION.

Scripture quotations noted The Message are from *The Message: The New Testament in Contemporary English.* Copyright © 1993 by Eugene H. Peterson.

ISBN 0-7852-6750-6

Printed in the United States of America

1 2 3 4 5 6 QWH 05 04 03 02 01 00

CONTENTS

I love Christmas. I love the music, the decorations, the traditions, the drama of the season. But sometimes Christmas can be a hurried, harried experience; we are too busy to catch our breath and realize that we are missing out on the precious, passing moments of our lives. Instead of finding pleasure in the celebration, we check our watches, scratch another activity off our "to do" list, and move on to the next thing. We constantly anticipate the future and do not appreciate the here and now. We go frantically from one thing to another, missing the point of Christmas altogether.

Christmas Abundance is about slowing down and savoring the sweetness of this wonderful season. It's about traditions old and new, honoring the sacred, celebrating the secular, and remembering the birth of the One whom this holiday is named after. It is about loving life in the here and now, rediscovering childhood wonder, and making each moment count. It's about taking time to love one another and to hear God's message of love to us.

I've had a delightful time writing this little plum pudding of a book. I hope that it contains a little something for everyone to enjoy. If *Christmas Abundance* enables you to take the time to see, hear, taste, touch, and smell the delights of the season, and to feel the Christmas spirit in your heart, then this book will have fulfilled its destiny.

May your Christmases be many and blessed.

Candy Paull

Invocation

Lord, be present with us now
as we come with tender hearts
to accept the Gift You bring.
Open our ears that we might hear.
Open our eyes that we might see.
Speak to us that we might know
the true meaning of this blessed Christmas season
that we may share in the inheritance of the saints
and find true peace among all peoples.
Glory be to God
who comes to us
and dwells with us,
Emmanuel.
May this Christmas be celebrated in love, joy, and peace
in our homes and around the world.
In the name of the Father,
the Son,
and the Holy Spirit.
Amen

PART 1

*T*HE SPIRIT OF THE SEASON

It is in the old Christmas carols, hymns, and traditions—those which date from the Middle Ages—that we find not only what makes Christmas poetic and soothing and stately, but first and foremost what makes Christmas exciting. The exciting quality of Christmas rests on an ancient and admitted paradox. It rests upon the paradox that the power and center of the whole universe may be found in some seemingly small matter, that the stars in their courses may move like a moving wheel around the neglected outhouse of an inn.

—G. K. CHESTERTON

It is good to be children sometimes, and never better than at Christmas,
when its mighty Founder was a child Himself.
—CHARLES DICKENS

Abundance is . . . Christmas Eve candlelight service.

For to you is born this day in the city of David a Savior,
who is Christ the Lord.
—LUKE 2:11 (RSV)

Abundance is . . . the sparkle of ornaments on evergreen branches.

Christmas is the season for kindling the fire of hospitality in the hall, the
genial flame of charity in the heart.
—WASHINGTON IRVING

Abundance is . . . going over the hill to Grandmother's house.

Abundance is . . . the scent of Douglas fir.

Christmas begins with anticipation. The child in all of us yearns for the beautiful gifts this season brings. Remember when you were a child, waiting for Christmas morning when all the glories of wrapped presents, filled stockings, lighted trees, and family feasts would be revealed? Often, when we become adults, we lose that childlike expectancy. Christmas sometimes seems more a chore to get through than a pleasure to savor. But the joyous simplicities of the season can still weave their magic, if we rediscover the eyes to see and the ears to hear.

Renew your sense of anticipation. Acknowledge the yearning of your heart through the symbols of Advent, where the church awaits the coming Redeemer. Feel the joy of Christmas morning, when the Gift is given and God has come to His people. And in Epiphany, honor the sacredness of life, as wise men and women through the ages have learned to do. Let a sense of anticipation renew your heart in this festive winter celebration.

Celebrate the abundance of Christmas by counting the blessings you have now and anticipating that the goodness you choose to experience today is a sign of the goodness you will experience tomorrow. Take the time to savor the delights of this season—and you will rediscover the joys of anticipation.

We are not to make the ideas of contentment and aspiration quarrel,
for God made them fast friends. A man may aspire,
and yet be quite content until it is time to rise;
and both flying and resting are but parts of one contentment.
The very fruit of the gospel is aspiration.
It is to the heart what spring is to the earth,
making every root, and bud, and bough desire to be more.

—HENRY WARD BEECHER

This is Christmas; not the tinsel, not the giving and receiving, not even the carols, but the humble heart that receives anew the wondrous gift, the Christ.

—FRANK MCKIBBON

What is the best gift you've ever received? What is the most memorable Christmas you've ever had? The best gifts are not the most expensive gifts. Sometimes a gift can be an affirmation of a dream we have, such as a set of paints, a pair of ballet shoes, a guitar, season tickets to the symphony, or tuition for a class we have been longing to attend. Other times, a gift can be a celebration of the beauty of our lives: a hand-painted silk scarf, a bouquet of roses, a fine handmade mahogany box, an antique clock that still keeps time perfectly. The most delightful gifts are the ones that are wrapped with love, thoughtfully chosen with the heart's desire in mind.

And the very best gift of all? Isn't it when we give and receive something of ourselves? Just as God gave His very best gift, His only Son, so this Christmas, let us give the gift of ourselves—our time, our talents, our energy, our attention—to each other in this Christmas season.

The best thing to give to your enemy is forgiveness; to an opponent, tolerance; to a friend, your heart; to your child, a good example; to a father, deference; to your mother, conduct that will make her proud of you; to yourself, respect; to all men, charity.

—FRANCIS MAITLAND BALFOUR

7

The things we do at Christmas are touched with a certain extravagance . . .

—ROBERT COLLYER

Christmas is like life: too religious for the secularist and too secular for the religious. Christmas as it has been celebrated through the centuries has always swung between legalism and license, celebration and contemplation, social acceptance and rejection by church or state. Christmas seems to be too big and too complex for those who like to have their days neatly boxed, labeled, and pigeonholed. This holiday is too wild and untamed, never neatly fitting into anyone's paradigm.

For instance, the founder of Christmas begins life in a manger, crying like a baby. What respectable almighty, all-powerful deity would countenance such a basic beginning? Yet the Bible says that this baby born to poor parents in an obscure corner of the Roman Empire was God Himself come to earth in human flesh. There is great discomfort with the Incarnation and the virgin birth; secularists cry, "Impossible! Myth, superstition, religious fanaticism." Angels coming to shepherds, a star leading wise men from another country, dreams and visions and prophecies and miracles—it all sounds a little strange to those who live in a more utilitarian time. Medieval theologians debated how many angels could dance on the head of a pin; modern secularists won't even admit that angels might exist. Ancient prophecies and the claim that this Child is their fulfillment sound like fantasies in a world that has decided

that prophets are out of date and miracles can all be explained away. Christmas is a difficult time for those who want easy explanations.

The secularists are not the only ones who have problems with Christmas. There is the religious disapproval of too much frivolity and too many pagan traditions and too much money spent on too many pleasures. For example, the Puritans who settled in Massachusetts, in their zeal to make faith a deeper and more meaningful experience, tried to legislate Christmas away in 1659 by passing a decree that anyone caught observing Christmas in any way would be fined five shillings.

The ebb and flow of social approval has meant that in one era Christmas becomes a quiet, sober holiday only celebrated by the faithful few, while another era will think Christmas should be ushered in with wild revels and excessive noise. One era says that any celebration of a religious holiday is foolish and proclaims a utilitarian workday, business as usual, in its place. Another era complains of excessive sentimentality. Each era has its own take on this paradoxical holiday. The Renaissance saw a flowering of lighthearted carols and beautiful folk traditions. The Puritan era brought a more serious observance to the forefront, condemning the frivolity of other eras. The eighteenth century found rowdy ways to mark the holiday, with noisy and drunken revelry in the streets. It took the Victorian era to tame wild Christmas and bring both the Christian and pagan folk customs to meet at the family hearth. In a culture that almost worshiped the ideal of a pure childlike innocence, the Victorian Christmas flourished, enhanced by the goods made available to a growing middle class by the industrial revolution. And of course, our dear, adolescent twentieth century has celebrated Christmas with unparalleled commercial excess.

At the dawn of the twenty-first century, let us enjoy the paradox of a holiday that is both sacred and secular, Christian and pagan, worshipful and commercial. Let us choose to celebrate with mature faith and childlike hearts. Let us learn to see sanctity in the commonplace, delight in the details, and open our hearts to embrace the contradictions. Let us keep room in our hearts for both God and mankind, heaven and earth.

If you want to work for the kingdom of God, and to bring it, and enter into it, there is just one condition to be first accepted. You must enter into it as children, or not at all.

—JOHN RUSKIN

I choose to celebrate the sacred holiday and incorporate the riches of almost two thousand years of thought, theology, liturgy, and ceremony in my life. I also choose to make Christmas joyous by reveling in ancient traditions, folk customs, carols and songs, and lovely nonsense that may or may not have roots in pagan beliefs. I can sing "O Holy Night!" with as much joy as I can dance to "Jingle Bell Rock." I will also make time for quietness to meditate on the meaning of Christmas, to treasure memories of Christmases past, and to pray for future Christmas hopes.

I choose to be a child again at the sight of a lighted Christmas tree. I also choose to be a sophisticated adult, dressed up for a wonderful party. I'll shop in malls and worship in church. I'll spend money on a sinfully delicious chocolate truffle and write a check for my favorite charity. Christmas is a festival of light celebrated during the darkest part of the year. It's a frenzy of spending in a commercialized environment, and an opportunity to listen to wonderful choirs singing about the love of God for mankind, which is without price. It's a family reunion, good fellowship time, and the time when I feel most lonely in a crowd. Secular saints like Santa Claus and angels singing "Glory, hallelujah" in a starry night are both images I can live with. And I will especially remember the paradox of God come as a child to earth to lift us up to heaven's heights. I intend to revel in the paradox of Christmas, in all its glory and messiness. Care to join me?

Oh rich and various man! Thou palace of sight and sound, carrying in thy senses the morning and the night, and the unfathomable galaxy in thy brain, the geometry of the City of God; in thy heart, the power of love.

—RALPH WALDO EMERSON

This Satan's drink is so delicious, it would be a pity to let the infidels have exclusive use of it. We shall fool Satan by baptizing it and making it a truly Christian beverage."

—POPE CLEMENT III, AFTER HE SAMPLED THE NEW BEVERAGE

COFFEE, AND WAS ASKED TO DECLARE IT UNHOLY

All praise to Thee, eternal Lord,
Clothed in a garb of flesh and blood;
Choosing a manger for Thy throne,
While worlds on worlds are Thine alone.

Once did the skies before Thee bow,
A Virgin's arms contain Thee now;
Angels, who did in Thee rejoice,
Now listen for Thine infant voice.

A little child, Thou art our guest,
That weary ones in Thee may rest;
Forlorn and lowly is Thy birth,

That we may rise to heaven from earth.
Thou comest in the darksome night,
To make us children of the light,
To make us in the realms divine,
Like Thine own angels, 'round thee shine.

All this for us Thy love hath done,
By this to Thee our love is won,
For this we tune our cheerful lays,
And shout our thanks in ceaseless praise.

MARTIN LUTHER (1483–1546)

TRANSLATOR: UNKNOWN, 1858

And he who gives a child a treat, makes joy-bells ring in heaven's sight.
—JOHN MASEFIELD

Abundance is . . . a wreath on the door.

Abundance is . . . eggnog in a cut-glass punch bowl.

Abundance is . . . the sound of children laughing.

The greatest gift that can come to anyone is to share in the infinite act by which God's love is poured out upon all men.
—THOMAS MERTON

Let every thing that hath breath praise the LORD.
Praise ye the LORD.
PSALM 150:6 (KJV)

Abundance is . . . antiques and tradition and gracious entertaining.

Abundance is . . . who I am, not what I own.

The abundant life is not one that is built around how much we own, how important we are in the world, or how much power and money we control. The abundant life is about appreciating the treasures that each moment offers us. It is about being able to take time for the essential things in life.

Christmas is a season for love, joy, and peace. But all too often we get caught up in the rush of events. As members of a society built around production and consumption, we often buy into the lie that too much is not enough. We stuff our schedules so full of activities that we have no spirit left to enjoy them. We spend our money for things we don't want or need. And though we try to fill our lives with what glossy magazines and television ads tell us we should have, somehow we always come up empty.

True abundance is a choice. We can choose to limit our activities and obligations so that we have time and energy to enjoy the gifts of the heart. We can choose to take time away from the false urgencies of our modern society and focus instead on the unforced rhythms of our humanity. Those who choose to practice true abundance realize that quantity time *is* quality time—human quality. Our bodies and minds need to have rest and quiet to enjoy the moments that count.

Take time for true abundance. Make choices that reflect the deepest needs of your heart, not the agendas of a world that lies to you and says that you are not enough. The message of Christmas says that through Christ we are enough and that eternal life is a gift from God, not a right we purchase. Each moment is a gift of grace—and true abundance is being aware of that.

Abundance is . . . time enough for love.

Abundance is . . . an open hand and a tender heart.

What good is it if I am a king and do not know I am a king?
—MEISTER ECKEHART

It is not what he has, nor even what he does, which directly expresses the worth of a man, but what he is.
—HENRI FREDERIC AMIEL

One of the most tragic things I know about human nature is that all of us tend to put off living. We are all dreaming of some magical rose garden over the horizon—instead of enjoying the roses that are blooming outside our window today.
—DALE CARNEGIE

The Victorians practically invented Christmas—at least the jolly Christmas we know today. Though Christmas has been celebrated since the fourth century, many of our modern customs were refined and popularized in the Victorian era. Ebenezer Scrooge, Santa Claus, Christmas trees, Christmas cards, advertising for shopping, caroling, and an emphasis on childhood and feasting around the family table all became an important part of Christmas in the nineteenth century.

Before the Victorians reinvented the season, Christmas was an occasion for drunken revels or was ignored completely. Loud bands of rowdies roamed the streets in "callithumpian bands," demanding treats while making noise. Puritans outlawed the holiday all together. Christmas was not even declared a holiday in the United States until the mid-1800s. The first state in the U.S. to make Christmas a legal holiday was Alabama, in 1836. Between 1850 and 1861, fifteen states followed suit. It wasn't until after the Civil War that schools, banks, and government offices closed for Christmas Day.

Victorian writers gave us a new vision of Christmas. Washington Irving wrote stories of feasting and family and Christmas in the early part of the century, including Saint Nicholas in his popular *Knickerbocker History*. His friend Clement Clarke Moore wrote "The Night Before Christmas," a poem that gave us a new version of Saint Nicholas who was a jolly old elf instead of an ancient saint. *Kris Kringle's Book*, written by an unknown author in 1842, told of a jolly, fat Saint Nicholas, or Kris

Kringle, who brought gifts to good little children. Then Charles Dickens brought us Ebenezer Scrooge and Tiny Tim and some of the most beloved Christmas stories of all time. How many towns today have a Dickens Christmas event that promotes local shops with costumed carolers and actors bringing life to the old *A Christmas Carol* cast of characters?

The Victorian era was especially child-centered, changing how children were viewed. In the eighteenth century children had been dressed like, and were expected to act like, small adults. The nineteenth century saw the rise of the nursery culture, which revolved around childhood. Victorian portrayals of childhood were romanticized, reflecting the ideals of the time and symbolizing childhood as a time of hope, optimism, and limitless potential. Some of the greatest children's books ever written were part of the flowering of the Victorian literary sentiments about the wonder and purity of childhood. The Victorian Christmas was tailor-made for the child—whatever the age of those who celebrated. Family traditions flourished. Parties especially for children were created; Christmas Eve and birthdays became the chief excuses for gifts, games, and goodies.

Queen Victoria and Prince Albert and their five children brought an air of domesticity to the culture. The royal family was reported on in the popular press, and during the middle of the century at the height of the British Empire, their lives offered a family portrait that traveled around the world.

Both conservative and romantic, the Victorians embraced the ideal of the family gathered round the hearth. "Home sweet home" was a sentiment

17

embroidered on the hearts and minds of a great majority of the populace. The Victorians gave us family evenings in the parlor, singing around the piano, or playing games. Some of our favorite Christmas carols were written during this time. For example, "Silent Night" was written in 1818, and "Jingle Bells," written in 1857, was a true Victorian creation. Other carols include "It Came upon the Midnight Clear" (1851) and "We Three Kings of Orient Are" (1859).

Christmas cards began showing up in England by the middle of the century, but it was Louis Prang who introduced America to the finest Christmas cards and made them popular in the 1870s. His beautiful chromolithographic, full-color printed cards are collector's items today. Christmas had always included charity for the poor, but now gift giving became central. "Christmas wouldn't be Christmas without presents," Jo said in Louisa May Alcott's classic, *Little Women*. Presents came to mean shopping—and a growing commercialism. As Christmas trees and decorations increased in popularity, the inventions of the industrial revolution made them available to a growing middle class.

Christmas shopping got its commercial edge from the Victorians. As early as the 1830s, newspapers were filled with print ads urging shoppers to consider buying everything from raisins for baked goods to pianofortes for the parlor to uplifting books for the mind, and more. By 1850 Santa Claus began to appear in stores and on street corners. Once the Victorians discovered the joys of shopping, there was no returning to a "simpler" time.

I wonder if you have ever read Dickens's Christmas books?
I have only read two yet, but I have cried my eyes out.

—ROBERT LOUIS STEVENSON

I now have my house full for Christmas holidays,
which I trust you also keep up in the good old style.

—WASHINGTON IRVING

Abundance is . . . a rich plum pudding full of sweetness and spice.

And it was always said of him that he knew how to keep Christmas well,
if any man alive possessed the knowledge.

—CHARLES DICKENS

Christmas trees have been around for at least four hundred years in one form or another. The tradition took root in Northern European cultures, where the evergreen was already regarded as a symbol of immortality. One lovely legend has it that the evergreen stood bashfully behind all the fruit- and flowering-trees that came to offer their gifts to the Christ child in the manger. Ashamed that it had no fruit or flower to bring, but only unchanging green branches, the evergreen stayed in the back of the crowd. But the stars saw how sad the tree was and took pity on the evergreen by coming down from heaven to nestle in its branches so that the simple evergreen might become the brightest of all the trees in creation.

Today's Christmas tree is decorated with long-burning electric lights and mass-produced ornaments. Most Christmas trees before the 1880s were decorated with handmade ornaments, fruits, nuts, and anything that could be created from scraps. Candles were lit for only a brief half hour on Christmas Eve. While children oohed and ahhed at the wonder of a lighted tree, nervous adults kept buckets of water handy in case of fire, which often happened. It wasn't until the 1920s, when electric lights were manufactured, that a lighted tree could be enjoyed safely over the duration of the holidays.

THE PARADISE TREE

The first Christmas tree was called the Paradise Tree. It was a prop for the Paradise Play, one of the miracle plays of the fifteenth century. During the Middle Ages, when most of the populace could not read or write, miracle plays taught Bible stories and church doctrine. These plays were arranged in yearly cycles around the church calendar, starting with the story of Creation and climaxing with the life of Jesus. Beginning with simply retelling the Scripture stories, miracle plays became more dramatic, with extrabiblical dialogue and ribald jokes. In 1210 Pope Innocent III forbade the clergy to act in them; but that just made the plays more popular because common folk and traveling actors took over the parts.

The story of Adam and Eve in Paradise, one of the most popular plays, took place on December 24, designated by the church as Adam and Eve's feast day. The tree would stand in the middle of the village square, a ring of candles surrounding the decorated tree. The decorations were symbolic of the story: apples symbolized the forbidden fruit and mankind's fall, while white communion wafers stood for Jesus Christ and mankind's redemption. Red cherries were a reminder of the legend of the cherry tree, which bent down to offer cherries to a pregnant Mary when suspicious Joseph would not pick them for her. The tree was a symbol of God's grace. Though the miracle plays eventually went out of fashion, people of northern Europe took the Paradise Tree into their hearts and homes.

THE CHRISTBAUM

One of the next developments in the history of the Christmas tree was the Christbaum, literally the Christ Tree. This tree was popular in Germany, and by 1605 a visitor to Strasbourg wrote in his diary, "At Christmas time fir trees are set up in the rooms . . . and hung with roses cut from paper of many colors, apples, wafers, spangle-gold, and sugar." Roses were a popular symbol of the Virgin Mary in the seventeenth century and considered an emblem of love, grace, and beauty. Christ-bundles were also hung on the tree: packets of candy, sugarplums, and cakes. Pastries began to replace the communion wafers of old—brown dough pastries representing men and animals, white dough for angels, stars, flowers, and hearts.

THE JESSE TREE

The Jesse Tree is an Advent tradition that helped people remember the ancestry of Christ and prophecies concerning His coming. "But a shoot shall sprout from the stump of Jesse and from his roots a bud shall blossom," reads Isaiah 11:1. Jesse was the father of David, and Jesus was of the House of David in Jewish genealogy. The genealogy of a child was of utmost importance to biblical Jews, so Jesus' ancestry was an essential part of His claim to be the Messiah.

Each ornament for the Jesse Tree is painted with a picture that symbolizes an aspect of the messianic prophecies surrounding Christ.

These symbols are all taken from the Bible and usually a Scripture reading accompanies each ornament. An ornament will be added to the tree each day in Advent.

Here are a few of the symbols for the Jesse Tree:

- *The tablets of the law:* the law of Moses, which Christ came to fulfill
- *The key of David:* a symbol of authority and power
- *The root of Jesse:* Christ as the descendant of the root of Jesse
- *The star of David:* the emblem of the royal house of David
- *Jonah in the whale:* as Jonah was in the whale three days, so Jesus was in the grave three days before His resurrection
- *The burning bush:* the bush encountered by Moses that burned but was not consumed also became a symbol of the virgin birth
- *Noah's ark:* Christ as the Ark who brings us safely through God's judgment
- *The apple:* the symbol of the fall from Eden and of the new Adam, Christ, who redeems us from the Fall
- *The Paschal Lamb:* a symbol for atonement, fulfilled by Christ as the Lamb of God who takes away the sins of the world
- *Manna:* Christ as true bread from heaven

Abundance is . . . picking out a Christmas tree.

THE ENGLISH TREE

We owe the widespread popularity of the Christmas tree in England and America to Prince Albert, Queen Victoria's beloved German husband. When Victoria and Albert married and started a family, Albert brought some of the customs from his homeland to England. Out of nostalgia for the jolly German traditions of Christmas, he put up a Christmas tree in Windsor Castle in 1841, the year after his first son, Edward VII, was born. Later, in a letter to his parents in Germany, he wrote, "Today I have two children of my own to make gifts to, who, they know not why, are full of happy wonder at the German Christmas tree and its radiant candles."

In December 1848, an engraving of the royal family gathered around a "German tree" was published in the *Illustrated London News*. The picture caused an immediate sensation, and soon the decorated tree was a popular part of the English Christmas celebration. Two years later *Godey's Lady's Book* published the picture in America, and the Christmas tree, already popular in German immigrants' homes, became universally accepted in the United States.

Prince Albert's tree was about five feet high and stood on a white, damask-covered table. Filled with the richest, most expensive sweets, the tree was topped by an angel holding wreaths in her outstretched hands. And underneath the tree and around the table were candy boxes, dolls, pull toys, and treasures to delight any child's heart.

THE CHRISTMAS TREE IN AMERICA

The Christmas tree took several forms in America, thanks to the different immigrants who brought favorite traditions from their homelands. The Pennsylvania Dutch decorated their trees with homemade ornaments and goodies. By the 1820s, decorated trees were a common sight in Pennsylvania Dutch country. They baked a veritable Noah's ark of animal cookies and Matzebaum, a rectangular cake of almond paste, sugar, and egg whites made by being pressed into a wooden mold, baked, and then painted with bright vegetable dyes. Springerle cookies were also favorites for hanging on the tree. Strings of dried apples, popcorn, raisins, and almonds garlanded the branches, while homemade stuffed animals, decorated hollow eggshells, carved toys, and small family presents like handkerchiefs, collars, little dolls, and other toys hung on the tree. Underneath, a manger scene, a gingerbread house, and baskets filled with straw awaited the *Christkind*, or Christ child, who would fill the baskets with toys for good girls and boys.

By the 1840s the decorated tree had become popular in the South. One of the first decorated trees was put up in Williamsburg, Virginia, in 1842. In 1850 the ladies of Charleston honored Jenny Lind with a Christmas tree in front of her hotel. Antebellum Southerners decorated their trees with strings of cranberries and popcorn, gilded pinecones, paper ornaments, tiny wreaths, and fruits and candies.

25

The Germans made the greatest contribution to the decorating of the Christmas tree. They invented the glass Christmas ball. The first ones were thick-walled glass balls called *Kugeln,* or kugels. In the 1870s, a glassmaker named Louis Greiner-Schlottfeger discovered how to blow paper-thin glass and developed a formula to silver the inside of the ornaments. The town of Lauscha in Germany specialized in these gorgeous glass ornaments and produced hundreds of thousands of ornaments between 1870 and 1930.

In the later part of the nineteenth century, stores like Woolworth's and Sears began carrying manufactured ornaments for sale. Edible and handmade ornaments were replaced by glass balls, elaborate cardboard figures, tinsel, glass beads, chromolithographic pictures, cotton-batting Santas and angels, and colorful gelatin lanterns, the forerunner of the electric Christmas tree light. In the 1920s and 1930s the electric Christmas tree light was being mass-produced, and American and Asian mass-produced glass balls began to replace the handblown German glass balls in popularity. Today there is a renaissance in the old way of hand-blowing Christmas ornaments, and an endless array of splendid decorations is available to make the evergreen branches twinkle and shine.

Abundance is . . . tinsel and twinkling lights.

Every child comes with the message that
God is not yet discouraged with man.

—RABINDRANATH TAGORE

Christmas is the child's holiday. The starry-eyed wonder of seeing the decorated tree, all sparkling with lights and ornaments twinkling on the branches and mysterious packages underneath. Little hands helping with the Christmas baking. Expectant hearts wide awake on Christmas Eve, knowing that going to sleep, the very thing they can't do, is the thing that brings the much anticipated Christmas morning. The adult finds a young heart again and the spirit is renewed when Christmas is seen through the eyes of a child.

May each Christmas, as it comes, find us more and more like Him who at
this time became a little child, for our sake, more simple-minded, more
humble, more affectionate, more resigned, more happy, more full of God.

—JOHN HENRY NEWMAN

Abundance is . . . shepherds in bathrobes and angels with dirty faces.

THE SUGAR-PLUM TREE

Have you ever heard of the Sugar-Plum Tree?
'Tis a marvel of great reknown!
It blooms on the shore of the Lollypop Sea
In the garden of Shut-Eye Town;
The fruit that it bears is so wondrously sweet
(As those who have tasted it say)
That good little children have only to eat
Of that fruit to be happy next day.

When you've got to the tree, you would have a hard time
To capture the fruit which I sing;
The tree is so tall that no person could climb
To the boughs where the sugar-plums swing!
But up in that tree sits a chocolate cat,
And a gingerbread dog prowls below—
And this is the way you contrive to get at

Those sugar-plums tempting you so:
You say but the word to that gingerbread dog
And he barks with such a terrible zest
That the chocolate cat is at once all agog,
As her swelling proportions attest.
And the chocolate cat goes cavorting around
From this leafy limb to that,
And the sugar-plums tumble, of course, to the ground—
Hurrah for that chocolate cat!

There are marshmallows, gumdrops, and peppermint canes
With stripings of scarlet and gold,
And you carry away of the treasure that rains,
As much as your apron can hold!
So come, little child, cuddle closer to me
In your dainty white nightcap and gown,
And I'll rock you away to that Sugar-Plum Tree
In the garden of Shut-Eye Town.

—EUGENE FIELD

Our religion is one which challenges the ordinary human standards by holding that the ideal of life is the spirit of a little child. We tend to glorify adulthood and wisdom and worldly prudence, but the Gospel reverses all this. The Gospel says that the inescapable condition of entrance into the divine fellowship is that we turn and become as a little child.

—ELTON TRUEBLOOD

Abundance is . . . a bicycle or a big doll under the tree.

Abundance is . . . a game of charades.

Abundance is . . . red-and-white-striped candy canes.

A baby is God's opinion that life should go on.
Never will a time come when the most
marvelous recent invention is as
marvelous as a newborn baby.

—CARL SANDBURG

The Yule trees and the dreams all children dream
The tremulous glow of candles in rows
The gold and silver of angels and globes
And the splendor of tinsel and toys under trees.

—BORIS PASTERNAK

Abundance is . . . stockings stuffed with toys, oranges, and candy.

Oh, how nice it would be, just for today and tomorrow, to be a little boy
of five instead of an aging playwright of fifty-five and look forward to all
the high jinks with passionate excitement and be given a clockwork train
with a full set of rails and a tunnel.

—NOEL COWARD

Abundance is . . . the sound of a toy train running on its tracks.

Abundance is . . . the "Dance of the Sugarplum Fairy" in the
Nutcracker Suite.

Abundance is . . . reading together Luke's account of the
Christmas story.

THE TOYS

My Little Son, who look'd from thoughtful eyes
And moved and spoke in quiet grown-up wise,
Having my law the seventh time disobey'd,
I struck him and dismiss'd
With hard words and unkiss'd,
—His Mother, who was patient, being dead.
Then, fearing lest his grief should hinder sleep,
I visited his bed,
But found him slumbering deep,
With darken'd eyelids, and their lashes yet
From his late sobbing wet.
And I, with moan,
Kissing away his tears, left others of my own;
For on a table drawn beside his head,
He had put, within his reach,
A box of counters and a red-vein'd stone,
A piece of glass abraded by the beach,
And six or seven shells,
A bottle with bluebells,
And two French copper coins, ranged there with careful art,
To comfort his sad heart.

So when that night I pray'd
To God, I wept and said:
Ah, when at last we lie with tranced breath,
Not vexing Thee in death,
And Thou rememberest of what toys
We made our joys,
How weakly understood
Thy great commanded good,
Then, fatherly not less
Than I whom Thou has moulded from the clay,
Thou'lt leave Thy wrath, and say,
"I will be sorry for their childishness."

—COVENTRY PATMORE

Abundance is . . . a story before bedtime.

Abundance is . . . the star on the top of the Christmas tree.

NATURE

As a fond mother, when the day is o'er,
  Leads by the hand her little child to bed,
  Half-willing, half-reluctant to be led,
  And leaves his broken playthings on the floor,
Still gazing at them through the open door,
  Nor wholly reassured and comforted
  By promises of others in their stead,
  Which, though more splendid, may not please him more
So Nature deals with us, and takes away
  Our playthings one by one, and by the hand
  Leads us to rest so gently, that we go
Scarce knowing if we wish to go or stay,
  Being too full of sleep to understand
  How far the unknown transcends the what we know.

—HENRY WADSWORTH LONGFELLOW

PRAYER

Dear Lord and Father of mankind,
  Forgive our foolish ways!
Reclothe us in our rightful mind,
In purer lives Thy service find,
  In deeper reverence, praise.

Drop Thy still dews of quietness,
  Till all our strivings cease;
Take from our souls the strain and stress,
And let our ordered lives confess
  The beauty of Thy peace.

—JOHN GREENLEAF WHITTIER

PRAYER AT NIGHT

O Lord, support us all the day long, until the shadows lengthen and the evening comes, and the busy world is hushed, and the fever of life is over, and our work is done. Then in thy mercy grant us a safe lodging, and a holy rest, and peace at the last. Amen

—FROM THE BOOK OF COMMON PRAYER

The air is filled with the pungent fragrance of lavender, wild mint, and thyme, blending with the gentle perfume of jasmine, honeysuckle, myrtle, and orange blossom, and the invigorating scent of Mediterranean pines carried on a sea-touched breeze. It is a long way from the North Pole residence of Santa Claus to the beautiful coastal area of Turkey where Saint Nicholas lived in the fourth century A.D. Gemiler Island on the Blue Coast of Turkey has also been known as Saint Nicholas Island, in honor of the ancient bishop of Myra. He became Noel Baba to the Turks, Father Christmas to Western Europeans, and eventually Santa Claus to the Americans.

A kind and benevolent bishop, Saint Nicholas was a popular figure in folk legend after his death. The earliest written accounts date from about five hundred years after his lifetime, so it is difficult to separate fact from fiction. He was born in what is now modern-day Turkey in approximately A.D. 280. His noble Christian parents left him an orphan with great wealth, which he gave away to the poor. He was selected bishop of the seaport town of Myra and was much loved by the people he shepherded. He suffered imprisonment and torture under the emperor Diocletian. His death has been placed at around 342 on December 6, which is still celebrated as Saint Nicholas Day in many countries.

The remains of saints in ancient times were considered important for popular worship. Saint Nicholas's bones were said to give off a sweet-smelling healing ointment. In 1087 the saint's remains were moved from Myra to Bari by a group of Italian merchants who probably felt that Saint Nicholas would be good for business. It was this move of the relics of the saint that caused the cult of Nicholas to grow rapidly throughout the west. Soon liturgies were created in his honor and were very popular up until the Reformation, when saints became less central in the worship of both Protestant and Catholic churches.

Saint Nicholas was known for his good works and mercy toward others. He provided three purses of gold for three penniless virgins so that they might have a marriage dowry rather than be sold into prostitution. Later legends claimed he threw these bags of gold down the chimney and they landed in stockings hung by the fire to dry. The three bags of gold were later symbolized by three balls of gold, the traditional sign over the door of a pawnbroker. The good Saint Nicholas became the patron saint of pawnbrokers and bankers because of a settlement with a dishonest broker. But bankers were not the only ones to benefit from Saint Nicholas's patronage.

Being bishop of a coastal town, Saint Nicholas became the patron saint of sailors, as well. In maritime tradition, sailors in the Ionian and Aegean Seas wished each other a good voyage with the phrase, "May Saint Nicholas hold the tiller," and steered by the "star of Nicholas."

Stories of seas being calmed, seamen being rescued, and multiplying grain in times of famine are only a few of the legends that accumulated around his name. He was said to have resurrected three boys, who were murdered by a butcher, taking them out of a vat of brine. In the way of folk legends, pretty soon that meant that a gift of crisp pickles was appropriate to celebrate the saint's day.

Saint Nicholas was especially known as a gift giver and lover of children. Because of his reputation as a preserver of sailors, Nicholas was honored in Normandy, Holland, and other seafaring places. A popular cultural representation became Father Christmas, or Sinte Klaas, who brought fruits, nuts, and little toys to good boys and girls on his feast day, December 6. Throughout the rest of Europe, Saint Nicholas Day became a feast day amid the fasting of Advent. In Scandinavia, it became a day for hospitality and visitation. Dutch immigrants brought him to America's shores and combined him with the German image of a *Christkind*, or Christ child. He became *Christ Kindel*, or Kris Kringle, in America.

In 1823 Clement Moore, an American minister and friend of Washington Irving, published the poem "The Night Before Christmas." Santa Claus became "chubby and plump, a right jolly old elf." In Thomas Nast's illustration of the poem in *Harper's Weekly* in 1863, we see a familiar, modern Santa Claus. The final touches on the image of Santa Claus were the illustrations done by the artist Haddon Sundblom for the Coca-Cola company in 1931. By the middle of the twentieth century a fourth-century bishop had become a benign, godlike, white-bearded grandfather.

In the paradoxical spirit of the sacred and secular holiday, Saint Nicholas and Santa Claus are icons of the Christmas we celebrate—its mysteries and its foolishness. I was raised with stories of Santa filling my stockings, but it was no great trauma to discover that my mother and father had bought the presents and filled my red flannel stocking (especially sewn for Christmas and hung by the mantel with care every Christmas Eve). I remember we three girls bouncing on my parents' bed, pulling gold chocolate coins and books of LifeSavers candies out of our stockings, a preliminary to opening the pile of presents under the tree. I'm still glad I left cookies and milk for Santa Claus, and I'm sure that Saint Nicholas received the gift in the spirit in which it was made.

Francis P. Church said it best when he wrote an editorial in the *New York Sun* in 1897. He told eight-year-old Virginia O'Hanlon, "Yes, Virginia, there is a Santa Claus. He exists as certainly as love and generosity and devotion exist . . . The most real things in the world are those that neither children nor men can see . . . there is a veil covering the unseen world which not the strongest man, nor even the united strength of all the strongest men that ever lived, could tear apart. Only faith, fancy, poetry, love, romance, can push aside that curtain and view and picture the supernal beauty and glory beyond." I choose to believe in fairy tales, to look at life through the eyes of a poet—and when I do I discover eternal truths that mere facts can never explain. Call me a hopeless romantic, but I will be happy to believe in that secular saint and holy fool, whether he be called Saint Nicholas or Santa Claus.

〇〇〇   〇〇〇   〇〇〇

The truth is more important than the facts.
—FRANK LLOYD WRIGHT

My first and last philosophy, that which I believe in with unbroken certainty, I learnt in the nursery. I generally learnt it from a nurse; that is, from the solemn and star-appointed priestess at once of democracy and tradition. The things I believed most then, the things I believe most now, are the things called fairy tales.

—G. K. CHESTERTON

For the foolishness of God is wiser than men,
and the weakness of God is stronger than men.

—1 CORINTHIANS 1:25 (RSV)

EPIGRAM

Sir, I admit your general rule,
That every poet is a fool,
But you yourself may serve to show it,
That every fool is not a poet.

—SAMUEL TAYLOR COLERIDGE

WHEN I HEARD THE LEARN'D ASTRONOMER

When I heard the learn'd astronomer,

When the proofs, the figures,

   were ranged in columns before me,

When I was shown the charts and diagrams,

   to add, divide, and measure them,

When I sitting heard the astronomer where he lectured with

   much applause in the lecture-room,

How soon unaccountable I became tired and sick,

Till rising and gliding out I wander'd off by myself,

In the mystical moist night-air, and from time to time,

Look'd up in perfect silence at the stars.

—WALT WHITMAN

Know you what it is to be a child? . . .
It is to have a spirit yet streaming from the waters of baptism;
it is to believe in love, to believe in loveliness, to believe in belief.
—PERCY BYSSHE SHELLEY

With everyone born human, a poet—an artist—is born,
who dies young and who is survived by an adult.
—CHARLES-AUGUSTIN SAINTE-BEUVE

Jesus rejoiced in the Spirit and said, "I thank You Father, Lord of
heaven and earth, that You have hidden these things from the world's
wise and revealed them to children."
—LUKE 10:21 (AUTHOR'S PARAPHRASE)

It takes a long time to become young.
—PABLO PICASSO

Skepticism, as I said, is not intellectual only;
it is moral also; a chronic atrophy and disease of the whole soul.
—THOMAS CARLYLE

It is only with the heart that one can see rightly;
What is essential is invisible to the eye.
—ANTOINE DE SAINT-EXUPÉRY

Listen, my children, with the ear of your heart.
—SAINT BENEDICT

Abundance is . . . Ebenezer Scrooge shouting "Bah! Humbug!"

Abundance is . . . Tiny Tim saying "God bless us every one!"

Some people will never learn anything . . .
because they understand everything too soon.
—ALEXANDER POPE

The heart has its reasons, which reason does not know.
—BLAISE PASCAL

Miss Piggy hangs two hundred sprigs of mistletoe—
and I try to avoid them.

—KERMIT THE FROG

When the trees have shed their leaves and winter cold has sent the plant world to sleep, the mistletoe grows green up among the bare branches. A partial parasite, it makes some of its own food but also takes minerals from its host tree. In medieval times mistletoe was thought to be magical; people believed it could cure epileptic fits, dispel tumors, divine treasure, and keep witches away. It was also used as a fertility potion and aphrodisiac, from which the custom of kissing under the mistletoe supposedly grew. It is also said that a sprig of mistletoe was included in a wreath that used to hang in houses as a substitute for effigies of the Holy Family that were once displayed in medieval doorways. When someone entered the home, one kissed under the symbol of the Holy Family and was warmly welcomed with the embrace of Christian fellowship. So you can choose whether your kiss under the mistletoe is a holdover from a pagan belief or a remnant of a religious tradition. Pious or pagan, I'll enjoy a kiss under the mistletoe as an important part of my Christmas celebration.

Abundance is . . . kisses under the mistletoe.

One of the delights of Christmas is dressing up. The swish of taffeta, the sheen of satin, the patterned glow of moiré, the soft crush of velvet, and a swirl of lace make dressing up for a Christmas party a sensuous experience. Red, white, purple, black, green, and colors in a rainbow of patterns and textures make a Christmas party a rich tapestry for the senses.

I remember one Christmas outfit. I wore it in college, when I sang in the choir and we performed the *Messiah* at the Seattle Opera House. My mother had made me a beautiful floor-length, red-plaid taffeta full skirt that swished when I walked. I bought two blouses to wear with it: one white cotton with lace, the other a silky soft gray with gentle ruffles at the neck and cuffs. The skirt had an extra-wide waistband, so it gave a cummerbund effect. But I also had a black wool vest that could be worn with it. Black strappy shoes completed the outfit, and I felt dressed and ready for anything.

Tartan is popular at Christmastime, partly because our celebrations hark back to Queen Victoria's reign. Not only did she and Prince Albert bring the Christmas tree to popularity, but they also made all things Scottish popular when they built and decorated Balmoral Castle. Soon all of England was checking to see what their proper family tartan should be. And if one didn't care about historical accuracy, the new mass-produced plaids in brilliant jewel colors would still make a pretty outfit or a colorful bow for a green wreath.

Whether you buy a new dress or bring a favorite gown out from your closet for another bow, may you have dressing up in abundance for your Christmas holiday celebrations. And may every woman in a dazzling dress have a prince charming of an escort in a formal suit (or kilt, if ye happen to be a Scot)!

Abundance is . . . black patent-leather shoes, shiny and new and perfect.

Abundance is . . . the swish and swirl of skirts moving
around the dance floor.

Abundance is . . . diamond-drop earrings sparkling under the lights.

Abundance is . . . the scent of a rich perfume.

Beauty is God's handwriting.
—CHARLES KINGSLEY

I can't understand how a woman can leave the house without fixing her-
self up a little, if only out of politeness. And then, you never know, maybe
that's the day she has a date with destiny and it's best to be as
pretty as possible for destiny.
—COCO CHANEL

For lack of attention, a thousand forms of loveliness elude us every day.
—EVELYN UNDERHILL

Christmas can be a time of great beauty, when we can choose to heighten our awareness. Because so many childhood memories are wrapped up in Christmas, we renew those experiences year by year—consciously or unconsciously—by enjoying childhood's familiar sights, scents, sounds, and sensations. Though we may be serious grown-ups with bills to pay and work to do, our child's heart can be distracted by the thousand simple joys that life offers. Take advantage of this many-layered richness. Stop sometime during each day of December and set aside time just to be aware of all the sensory riches of this time of year. Think about the small bounties you have encountered, and open yourself to experience each moment more fully.

There are so many beauties to experience. A wreath on a door. The sound of the oven door opening and the fragrance of freshly baked sugar cookies. A turkey dinner. The crunch of snow underfoot. Christmas carolers in a downtown plaza. A lighted Christmas tree through the window. Eager children looking at a department store window display. Red roses in a florist's shop. The scent of expensive perfume from an elegantly dressed woman. Candles burning in a sanctuary. The mystery of brightly wrapped packages.

If you are too busy to be aware of these things, you are too busy. If you are too old to be a child again, you are too old.

In all ranks of life the human heart yearns for the beautiful;
and the beautiful things that God makes are his gift to all alike.

—HARRIET BEECHER STOWE

Looking for and enjoying beauty is a way to nourish the soul. The universe
is in the habit of making beauty. There are flowers and songs, snowflakes
and smiles, acts of great courage, laughter between friends, a job well done,
the smell of fresh-baked bread. Beauty is everywhere.

—MATTHEW FOX

Consider the lilies of the field, how they grow;
they neither toil nor spin;
yet I tell you, even Solomon in all his glory
was not arrayed like one of these.

—MATTHEW 6:28-29 (AUTHOR'S PARAPHRASE)

Abundance is . . . a dozen red Christmas roses.

Abundance is . . . a soloist who can really, really sing
"The Trumpet Shall Sound."

No moment is trivial since each one contains a
divine kingdom and heavenly sustenance.

—JEAN PIERRE DE CAUSSADE

49

PART 2

DVENT: A TIME OF PREPARATION

Dear Lord, give me the truths which are veiled by the doctrines and articles of faith, which are masked by the pious words of sermons and books. Let my eyes penetrate the veil, and tear off the mask, that I can see your truth face to face.

—SAINT JOHN OF THE CROSS

The Word of God, Jesus Christ, on account of his great love for mankind, became what we are in order to make us what he is himself.

—SAINT IRENAEUS

Therefore the Lord himself shall give you a sign; behold, a virgin shall conceive, and bear a son, and shall call his name Immanuel.

—ISAIAH 7:14 (KJV)

He has granted to us his precious and very great promises . . .

—2 PETER 1:4 (RSV)

Christmas is the fulfillment of promise. It is also the promise of fulfillment. Scriptures are read and the story of the birth of Christ is told. Prophecies that foretell the Messiah's birth find fulfillment in the stable scene at Bethlehem. Angels sing of peace on earth and goodwill toward men. Advent is a season of dwelling in the promise, awaiting the coming Christ. It is a time to meditate on the prophecies of a coming Redeemer and to long not only for the first advent of Christ, but to also wait expectantly for the Second Coming, when the whole earth will be healed and the lion and lamb will lie down in peace together.

For more than fifteen hundred years, Advent has been a time for Christians to think about God's promises and the longing for their fulfillment. The church liturgical year begins not with Christmas, but with our yearning for the promise in the Advent season. Advent is almost as old as the celebration of Christmas itself. It is a season of spiritual preparation that extends from the fourth Sunday before Christmas through Christmas Eve.

Advent is not well known as a season in our modern society. It tends to be lost in the secular holiday, and even many Christians do not know about this meaningful time when the church prepares for the coming of Christ into the world. Advent, like Lent, has always been a season of prayer and fasting. It is marked by prayer, works of mercy, and times of worship. But it is also a time of joyful anticipation. Let this anticipation grow in your own heart as you begin your Christmas preparations. Let the traditions of Advent help you make room for the gifts and surprises that God wants to give you.

᷈᷈᷈   ᷈᷈᷈   ᷈᷈᷈

HOPE

Hope, like a gleaming taper's light,
Adorns and cheers our way;
And still, as darker grows the night,
Emits a brighter ray.

—OLIVER GOLDSMITH

In your Christmas preparations, enjoy some of the stillness and expectancy of Advent. Think not only about messianic promises, but also about the personal promises of God that answer the cry of your heart, that speak to your deepest hopes and dreams. As you wrap gifts, bake cookies, sing carols, and gather with friends, let the spirit of Advent whisper secrets of love and peace and joy to your heart. Here are some simple ways to make Advent a meaningful part of your Christmas celebrations:

- Make a special offering for the needs of the poor. The Salvation Army Angel Tree offers a wonderful way to adopt a child or family and buy them the Christmas gifts they cannot afford. Or give your children the money to choose and buy a toy for a less fortunate child. Or make a special offering at your church or to a community organization.

- Set up a crèche, or manger scene.

- Buy an Advent calendar and open the windows day by day. There are many available for sale each year.

- Abstain from a favorite food two or more days a week as a reminder to leave space in your heart for the coming Christmas gift.

- Bake a special treat that will not be eaten until Christmas Day.

- Host a Christmas carol party and be sure to sing some of the songs of Advent, including "O Come, O Come, Emmanuel."

- Have each family member participate by picking a name out of a hat; the person whose name they select will be the secret "Christ child" for the one who has drawn the name. Each day try to do something loving for that person.

- Create an Advent wreath and light the Advent candles each Sunday.

- Take a few hours, or a day away, and meditate on what is important to you.

Even if it's a little thing, do something for those who have need of help, something for which you get no pay but the privilege of doing it.
—ALBERT SCHWEITZER

Happiness is the cheapest thing in the world when we buy it for someone else.
—PAUL FLEMING

December 25 has been celebrated as Christmas since the fourth century A.D. It was chosen by the early church for both practical and symbolic reasons. The pagan feast of the "Unconquered Sun God," or Sol Invictus, was celebrated at the winter solstice. And the days of Saturnalia, December 17 to 23, were also celebrated in Rome with wild abandon. The date was also astronomically significant, occurring as the winter sun began to move toward its zenith and people could see that the circle of seasons would continue into the new life of spring. The church replaced many pagan and folk holidays with Christian holy days. Often the old meanings of the holidays carried into the new holy days, creating new forms and traditions.

Epiphany was celebrated starting in the second century, and by the mid sixth century, the Twelve Days of Christmas, from Christmas Day to Epiphany, became a sacred and festive season. The Eastern Church celebrated the birth of Christ on January 6, while December 25 became the day of celebration in the Western church. For many centuries this season has been celebrated by music, caroling, Christmas plays, feasting, holding open house, charity to the poor, extra rations for animals, and gift giving.

Most scholars choose 6 or 7 B.C. for the actual year of Christ's birth. Dionysius Exigus, a sixth-century monk, wanted to number the years of history based on the year of Jesus Christ's birth. Due to insufficient historical data, he was a few years off the mark, and his mistake persists in our calendars today.

Scholars speculate that the birth took place in the spring, rather than the winter. From November to Passover, in March or April, the sheep were under cover to protect them from rain and cold weather. Because Luke mentions that the shepherds were out in the field watching the sheep, it is very likely that the traditional date for Christmas is inaccurate. The stable that Mary and Joseph sheltered in could have been a cave where the sheep were kept during the winter months, and they would have found it empty in the spring of the year.

Whatever the actual date of the events, the symbolism of December 25 has become an indelible part of our history. We celebrate a holiday with human history and tradition behind it—and this season is richer because of the mysteries and miscalculations.

And in the sixth month the angel Gabriel was sent from God unto a city of Galilee, named Nazareth, to a virgin espoused to a man whose name was Joseph, of the house of David; and the virgin's name was Mary. And the angel came in unto her, and said, Hail, thou that art highly favoured, the Lord is with thee: blessed art thou among women. And when she saw him, she was troubled at his saying, and cast in her mind what manner of salutation this should be. And the angel said unto her, Fear not, Mary: for thou hast found favour with God. And, behold, thou shalt conceive in thy womb, and bring forth a son, and shalt call his name JESUS.

—LUKE 1:26–31 (KJV)

She was a young girl. Yet when the angel came, she was not afraid to say yes, even when confronted with an impossibility. Just as God chose the youngest son, David, to be the next king of Israel after Saul, so He often chooses people who seem to be the most unlikely, unworldly selection for a special work. God has a call for all of us—a call to conceive and bear our own dreams and tasks. We, too, can say yes to what He asks, even if we don't understand how it will be accomplished.

For with God nothing shall be impossible. And Mary said, Behold the handmaid of the Lord; be it unto me according to thy word.

—LUKE 1:37–38 (KJV)

Christmas is more than just a good time. In fact, statistics show that more people are depressed during the holidays than at any other time of year, partly because the shorter days and lack of sunlight can affect the temperament. But depression also comes from all the pressures to perform and the unmet expectations of a "perfect" Christmas that isn't humanly possible to achieve.

The images we see of happy families cheerily getting along together over a plump roast goose and groaning table may not be our personal reality. Instead, we often find ourselves with overburdened time schedules, family arguments, tight budgets, travel disasters, and loneliness. Christmas can be especially poignant after the loss of a loved one, when every tradition renewed cries out that the loved one is no longer here to share the joy. The heart aches with the difference between the happy image and the painful reality. Advent can be a meaningful and healing time for the hurting heart during the Christmas season.

Advent speaks to the deepest yearnings in our hearts, to the things that are broken, incomplete, unfulfilled. The darkness and longing are not avoided. They are brought out and honored, spoken to, and given room for acknowledgment. The acknowledgment of loss, of need, of longing, is deep in the Advent tradition. The mystery is allowed space to breathe—and so are we.

During Advent, we acknowledge that we do not have all the answers. We acknowledge that we are finite, mortal humans. We don't have to be "perfect" and neither does our family. We may be single, widowed, childless, or with a different kind of family than the Norman Rockwell paintings portray. It will still be all right. God is coming, and God is with us. Sometimes, that is all we have and all we really need, no matter what our situation.

We also acknowledge the anticipation of a promised eternal healing and binding of our wounds, seen as God enters into our pain, moving into the neighborhood and dwelling with us as Emmanuel, which means "God with us." Let the songs and traditions and Scriptures of Advent speak to your hungry heart. They will strengthen you to welcome the coming Light. Enter into Advent, accept that life is a mystery, and allow peace to steal into your soul.

If you do not hope, you will not find what is beyond your hopes.
—SAINT CLEMENT OF ALEXANDRIA

Abundance is . . . paperwhites opening up on a sunny
winter windowsill.

As a deer longs for flowing streams,
So yearns my soul for You, my God.

—PSALM 42:1 (AUTHOR'S PARAPHRASE)

O Lord, You have created us for Yourself,
and our hearts are restless until they rest in Thee.

—SAINT AUGUSTINE

Abundance is . . . Celtic harp concerts and storytellers.

Abundance is . . . evergreens and candles on the mantle.

Advent is primarily about the coming of God, and only in a
secondary way about our asking, seeking, waiting, and longing.
There is hope, because we are unconditionally loved,
whatever may be our failures, our tepidity, or our secret despair.

—MARIA BOULDING

Fine old Christmas, with the snowy hair and ruddy face, had done his duty that year in the noblest fashion, and had set off his rich gifts of warmth and color with all the heightening contrast of frost and snow.

—GEORGE ELIOT

Our images of Christmas include winter. Though Christmases in the southern hemisphere are celebrated in the heat of summer, the northern hemisphere's wintry cold is held deep in our collective imaginations. We sing about a "Winter Wonderland" and "Chestnuts Roasting on an Open Fire" and "Frosty the Snowman" and "Let It Snow, Let It Snow, Let It Snow." Our Christmas cards have sleighs and snowy landscapes, ice-skating scenes and cozy cottages covered in white. So many of the Christmas traditions that come down to us grew out of the Northern European experience of winter, so much so that it's hard to imagine Christmas without winter, even in warmer climates.

Abundance is . . . icicles hanging from the eaves.

Winter offers a powerful metaphor for the coldness of a world waiting. All the leaves are gone, the fields are naked, and the world seems to be frozen or sleeping. Winter is a time of stillness and yearning. It is a time to gather around the fire and to keep company with memories. Winter comes to our spirits as well, as we wait for a change of season and for God to enter our dark night of the soul and bring us healing light. Christmas is made even more lovely because its glowing warmth offers a rich contrast to long, cold nights and fallow fields.

Abundance is . . . the crunch of boots on snow.

There are winter mornings
when the cold without
only adds to the warm within,
and the more it blows,
brighter the fires blaze.
—EMILY DICKINSON

Abundance is . . . a Yule log burning in a huge fireplace.

63

Out of the bosom of the Air,
　　Out of the cloud-folds of her garments shaken,
Over the woodlands brown and bare,
　　Over the harvest-fields forsaken,
　　　Silent, and soft, and slow
　　　Descends the snow.

—HENRY WADSWORTH LONGFELLOW

I love the spare tree branches of winter, the empty branches reaching toward heaven. And when winter snow outlines the branches in white, sometimes I think my heart might break with the beauty.

I have known only brief encounters with snow. Winters in the Pacific Northwest were mostly moody gray and cedar green. Snow was in the mountains, but in the valleys the dark woods and pale fields brooded through the winter months. Here in my current home in the Southeast, winters are brighter but still subdued, with brown branches and tan grass against blue and pale gray skies. In both places, snow comes only once or twice a year and usually does not linger. I have not lived in a climate where snow comes to stay, so I have not grown jaded with the sight of dirty snow and half-frozen slush. Instead, I savor my snow encounters, because they only come for brief moments.

When a snowstorm comes, wonder arrives with it. Suddenly the landscape is transformed and purified. Colors are muted to shadows, and the shadows dance with sunlight and snow to create a black-and-white picture-postcard of winter. A mantle of white covers the contours of the land and, like a bride's dress of satin, the untouched snow glows with beauty. There is a metallic tang to the cold air and sounds are muffled and distant. The silent falling snow tastes wet on the tongue and touches my eyelashes with feather-fall flakes. I revel in the untouched purity of the scene. Soon the snow blanket will be covered with footprints and one day it will turn to slush and mud, but for a brief moment the world is enchanted in white.

Take long walks in stormy weather or through deep snow in the fields and woods, if you would keep your spirits up.

—HENRY DAVID THOREAU

Abundance is . . . a steaming cup of hot chocolate to welcome you in from the cold.

If December passes without snow, we indignantly demand to know what has become of our good, old fashioned winters, and talk as if we had been cheated out of something we had bought and paid for; and when it does snow, our language is a disgrace to a Christian nation.

—JEROME K. JEROME

Abundance is . . . evergreens bending in the snow.

Abundance is . . . snow falling softly from a heavy gray sky.

Again at Christmas did we weave
The holly round the Christmas hearth
The silent snow possessed the Earth
And calmly fell on Christmas Eve.

—ALFRED, LORD TENNYSON

Abundance is . . . sugarplums and candy kisses.

WINTER NIGHTS

Now winter nights enlarge
The number of their hours,
And clouds their storms discharge
Upon the airy towers.
Let now the chimney blaze
And cups o'erflow with wine;
Let well tuned words amaze
With harmony divine.
Now yellow waxen lights
Shall wait on honey love,
While youthful revels, masques, and courtly sights
Sleep's leaden spells remove.

—THOMAS CAMPION

Abundance is . . . a gorgeous, big wreath on the door.

Heap on more wood!—the wind is chill;
But let it whistle as it will,
We'll keep our Christmas merry still.

—SIR WALTER SCOTT

But Mary kept all these things, pondering them in her heart.

—LUKE 2:19 (RSV)

The beautiful paintings of the Madonna and child reflect a perfect picture of serenity. Through the ages, Mary, the mother of Jesus, has inspired images of devotion and quietness. With our concentration on getting and giving and decorating and partying, we see the contrast of our frazzled faces in the mirror to Mary's serene face in the paintings and wonder why. Isn't it time to take a moment to reflect?

It is a good thing to reflect on our lives this Christmas season, to put aside some hours and ponder in our hearts why we are celebrating in the first place. I know we're all busy. I know that for many, Christmas is a season full of family needs and obligations at work and community service. But of what use is it to do all these good things if we do not have time for the best, for the quiet rest we cannot live without?

One of the most meaningful times I've experienced was when I took a day for an Advent retreat. Scarritt-Bennett Center in Nashville offers a one-day retreat during the Advent season for whomever wants to come. From nine in the morning until around three in the afternoon, we set aside time to reflect on how we spend our hours, what we would like to do differently in those hours, and how we want to make our Christmases richer and quieter and more centered.

Every woman in the group shared personal thoughts and feelings about this season in their lives. Plenty of time was set aside for journaling and art exercises that spoke to the spirit. We enjoyed a Christmas buffet together. As the afternoon sun slanted in through the windows and we took Communion, I felt that a few wrinkles in my spirit had been ironed out. I came away stronger and more centered.

Many churches and spiritual centers offer Advent retreats. If you don't have something available in your area, create your own Advent retreat with a few hours away from the demands of your busy day. Go to a church and pray. Get together with a friend or two in a quiet place and read and reflect on where you are and what you want to experience this year. If weather permits, walk in a winter garden. Choose a quiet time one afternoon in your own house, put some music on, light a candle, sip some hot tea, and read a seasonal meditation and write in your journal. Make this a time just for you, to rediscover the serenity that is so easily lost in the rush of modern life. Ponder in your heart the questions and hopes and dreams that you don't normally give yourself time to think about. Like the serenity depicted by the Madonna in the portraits, you, too, can find a quiet moment to rediscover the serenity of the season.

Some questions to ask yourself on an Advent retreat:

- What new thing is being born in my life at this time?

- What work do I want to do with my whole heart?

- In what ways do I need to give myself a break and lighten up?

- What are my sources for renewal, for courage, and for finding fresh perspective?

- What needs to be let go? Who do I need to forgive?

- What brings me a sense of peace and serenity?

- How will I choose to make time and space for renewal?

Think of your talents as a gift from God. What will you do when you open your present? Will you delight in what you have received, sharing your joy with everyone you can? Will you peer into the box and say it doesn't fit or wasn't what you ordered? Will you return it? Give it away? Or, will you leave it—unopened and abandoned? To accept and use your gift is to honor the giver. Open your present. Use your talents. Honor God—and yourself.

—DONNA MICHAEL

No spiritual exercise is as good as that of silence.

—SAINT SERAPHIM OF SAROV

Our task is to listen to the news that is always arriving out of silence.

—RAINER MARIA RILKE

O LORD, my heart is not lifted up,
  my eyes are not raised too high;
I do not occupy myself with things
  too great and too marvelous for me.
But I have calmed and quieted my soul,
  like a child quieted at its mother's breast;
  like a child that is quieted is my soul.

—PSALM 131:1–2 (RSV)

Abundance is . . . a favorite book to read on a quiet winter afternoon.

The rooms were very still while the pages were softly
turned and the winter sunshine crept in to touch the bright
heads and serious faces with a Christmas greeting.

—LOUISA MAY ALCOTT, *LITTLE WOMEN*

*God is the friend of silence. See how nature—trees, flowers,
grass—grow in silence? The more we receive in silent prayer,
the more we can give in our active life.*

—MOTHER TERESA

*In the rush and noise of life, as you have intervals,
step within yourselves and be still. Wait upon God and feel his good
presence; this will carry you though your day's business.*

—WILLIAM PENN

Time is an education for eternity.

—AUTHOR UNKNOWN

Abundance is . . . a moment for reflection.

Abundance is . . . unpacking favorite Christmas ornaments.

THE MAGNIFICAT

My soul magnifies the Lord,

and my spirit rejoices in God my Savior,

for he has regarded the low estate of his handmaiden.

For behold, henceforth all generations will call me blessed;

for he who is mighty has done great things for me,

and holy is his name.

And his mercy is on those who fear him

from generation to generation.

He has shown strength with his arm,

he has scattered the proud in the imagination of their hearts.

he has put down the mighty from their thrones,

and exalted those of low degree;

he has filled the hungry with good things,

and the rich he has sent empty away.

He has helped his servant Israel,

in remembrance of his mercy,

as he spoke to our fathers,

to Abraham and to his posterity for ever.

—LUKE 1:46–55 (RSV)

O COME, O COME, EMMANUEL

O come, O come, Emmanuel,
And ransom captive Israel,
That mourns in lonely exile here,
Until the Son of God appear.

Chorus: Rejoice! Rejoice! Emmanuel shall come to thee O Israel.

O come, O Wisdom from on high,
Who orders all things mightily,
To us the path of knowledge show,
And teach us in her ways to go.

Chorus: Rejoice! Rejoice! Emmanuel shall come to thee O Israel.

O come, O come, thou Lord of might
Who to Thy tribes on Sinai's height
In ancient times didst give the law
In cloud and majesty and awe.

Chorus: Rejoice! Rejoice! Emmanuel shall come to thee O Israel.

O come, O Rod of Jesse, free
Thine own from Satan's tyranny;
From depths of hell Thy people save,
And give them victory o'er the grave.

Chorus: Rejoice! Rejoice! Emmanuel shall come to thee O Israel.

O come, thou Key of David, come,
And open wide our heavenly home;
Make safe the way that leads on high,
And close the path to misery.

Chorus: Rejoice! Rejoice! Emmanuel shall come to thee O Israel.

O come, thou Dayspring, come and cheer
Our spirits by Thine advent here;
Disperse the gloomy clouds of night,
And death's dark shadows put to flight.

Chorus: Rejoice! Rejoice! Emmanuel shall come to thee O Israel.

O come, Desire of Nations, bind
In one the hearts of all mankind:
Bid Thou our sad divisions cease,
And be thyself our King of peace.

Chorus: Rejoice! Rejoice! Emmanuel shall come to thee O Israel.

—WORDS: LATIN, C. NINTH CENTURY

TRANSLATOR: JOHN M. NEALE

All the goods of this world . . . are finite and limited and radically incapable of satisfying the desire that perpetually burns within us for an infinite and perfect good.

—SIMONE WEIL

Not everything that counts can be counted and not everything that can be counted counts.

—ALBERT EINSTEIN

In an age obsessed with numbers, money, measurements, and a utilitarian view of human beings as consumers and producers, Christmas has often been reduced to a merely commercial enterprise. While there is nothing wrong with making things, buying and selling, and choosing the best for those we love, we have to make a conscious choice not to be caught up in it all. We are bombarded with messages that manufacture desires, and advertisers tell us we are incomplete unless we buy their product—often a product we didn't even know existed until they told us we needed it. We are reduced to the role of consumer, with an emphasis on what we lack.

There is an image from China of this constant hunger without fulfillment. The hungry ghost has a huge stomach and a small mouth. It can never be satisfied, but is only eternally empty. The mouth can never take in as much as the stomach desires. Sometimes it seems that the American experience of Christmas is one where hungry ghosts try to fill the heart's emptiness with things that do not satisfy. I have worked in retail businesses that depend on Christmas buying for a third or more of their yearly profits. I know the reality of being in business—it's good when people come and buy your merchandise. But when Christmas is measured only by goods bought and sold, something is wrong.

The world measures a nation's worth by Gross Domestic Product (GDP). Created during World War II, the GDP concept grew out of a system to keep track of the resources necessary to wage war. Using a model that calculated all goods and services bought and sold each year, it became the standard by which we measured the relative wealth of nations. But what is measured—and what is not measured—skews the picture. The Gross Domestic Product does not measure life's most meaningful moments.

According to the GDP formula, a woman who cares for her children, cooks healthful meals, and makes love with her husband adds no value to the GDP because she earns no money doing so. A family that bakes cookies, wraps presents, decorates the tree, and goes to Christmas Eve worship service is only valued by the price they paid for the tree and the cookie ingredients, the gas they used to drive to church, and the cost of the wax in the candles they light on the eve of the Son's birth. The faith, love, and hope behind those actions are meaningless when measured only by the Gross Domestic Product.

Children and dogs are as necessary to the welfare of the country as Wall Street and the railroads.

—HARRY S. TRUMAN

Figures lie and liars figure.

—WALL STREET JOURNAL

You can't worship two gods at once. Loving one god, you'll end up
hating the other. Adoration of one feeds contempt for the other. You
can't worship God and Money both.

—MATTHEW 6:24 *(THE MESSAGE)*

A lie which is half a truth is ever the blackest of lies.

—ALFRED, LORD TENNYSON

How often do we weigh and measure our lives by a similar standard? We
devalue the treasure we do have when we weigh our lives by the world's
standards of productivity. We unconsciously buy into a system that values the price of a gift, not the heart's intention. We buy into this num-
bers-oriented worldview, not realizing how much it colors our own
values. It's easy to put a price on something that can be weighed, measured, and exchanged. It is more difficult to put a value on a merciful
spirit and a tender heart.

For I have no pleasure in the death of any one,
says the Lord God; so turn, and live.

—EZEKIEL 18:32 (RSV)

This is an age-old problem. It is reflected in the birth story of Jesus Christ. The Roman emperor decrees a census. "Head 'em up, move 'em out. Caesar needs a head count so he can collect more taxes." So Joseph and Mary make their way to Bethlehem to be counted. And by the tax man's measure, they do not count for very much. Joseph is a poor village carpenter. Mary is just a woman expecting a baby. And the infant? What can a poor person's child contribute to mighty Caesar? If the parents are rich enough to buy the latest baby carriage from the Ciceromart down the road, then the birth of their son might add to the Gross Domestic Product of the Roman Empire. Taxes are collected on goods made and sold, not on what a poor couple can't afford.

The Romans would have concluded that if God was going to make an appearance, you'd think He would choose a more upscale neighborhood than a stable in Bethlehem. Why would He bother with an obscure country on the fringes of the great Roman Empire when He could be born in mighty Rome, the capital of the known world?

Why is God so disinterested in contributing to the Gross Domestic Product? When you measure what happened in Bethlehem by the numbers, it doesn't add up. Ah, but when you measure it by the immeasurable riches of the spirit, then you find wealth that makes gold, diamonds, and rubies pale in comparison. There is no price that can be put on things of soul and spirit—or God's love for us.

Our bodies consist of a few cents' worth of water and minerals. They are also unfathomable wonders housing eternal, sacred souls. Christmas asks us to look at the real value of things every year. Though there is nothing wrong with goods and services sold and traded, that is only a part of the picture. The motivations of the heart, the reasons behind the buying and the selling, and the ability to look beyond the numbers to the heart of the matter are in the end the only things that "count."

When you count your blessings at this Christmastide, remember that the impractical, impoverished couple in Bethlehem made room in their hearts for the mysteries of God while the practical Roman world didn't even know God was in their midst. Look into a child's eyes, and you'll find the true spirit of Christmas.

Measure success with a single word—love.

—GARRY MOORE

One who merely breathes, eats, sleeps, and works,
without awareness, without purpose and without ideas of his own is not
really a man. Life, in this purely physical sense, is merely the absence of
death. Such people do not live, they vegetate.

—THOMAS MERTON

If your everyday life seems poor, don't blame it; blame yourself; admit to
yourself that you are not enough of a poet to call forth its riches; because
for the creator there is no poverty and no poor indifferent place.

—RAINER MARIA RILKE

None of these things that go into making up what is distinctively and char-
acteristically human in us can be possessed—they all must be entered into.

—EUGENE PETERSON

We make a living by what we get;
We make a life by what we give.
—WINSTON CHURCHILL

Let me tell you why you are here. You're here to be salt-seasoning
that brings out the God-flavors of this earth.
If you lose your saltiness, how will people taste godliness?
You've lost your usefulness and will end up in the garbage.
—MATTHEW 5:13 *(THE MESSAGE)*

Those who have no inner life are prisoners of their surroundings.
—HENRI F. AMIEL

Ours is a culture based on excess, on overproduction; the result is a steady
loss of sharpness in our sensory experience.
—SUSAN SONTAG

Where were you when I laid the foundation of the earth?
  Tell me, if you have understanding.
Who determined its measurements—surely you know!
  Or who stretched the line upon it?
On what were its bases sunk, or who laid its cornerstone,
  when the morning stars sang together,
  and all the sons of God shouted for joy?

—JOB 38:4–7 (RSV)

Nobody has measured, even poets, how much a heart can hold.
—ZELDA FITZGERALD

Abundance is . . . young Queen Victoria and her new husband;
newlyweds sharing their very first
Christmas together and very much in love.

Abundance is . . . cozy chats by the fireside.

Better is a handful of quietness than two hands
full of toil and a striving after wind.

—ECCLESIASTES 4:6 (RSV)

Consider the lilies of the field, how they grow;
they neither toil nor spin; yet I tell you,
even Solomon in all his glory was not arrayed like one of these.

—MATTHEW 6:28–29 (RSV)

The way of Advent speaks to the need we all have for rest. Advent is not just a collection of ceremonies and traditions that we perform. This is a time that you can choose to rest in your life, to savor it. You can allow the commercialism and hustle-bustle of the holiday to take over your life. Or you can choose to celebrate a Sabbath of the spirit.

I recommend turning the four Sundays of Advent into a retreat, a real Sabbath break from your usual routine. Go to church. Then come home and light some candles, fix a homemade dinner, go for a walk, read the funny papers, and spend time with those you love. It sounds so simple, doesn't it? But if your Sunday is scheduled to be just as crowded as your weekdays, it takes a new skill to learn how to slow down and just be.

It is very countercultural to make this choice, because the world shouts at you that you must do, do, do, and buy, buy, buy. You can choose to slow down, clear out your schedule, live without crossing another thing off your list of things to do. Retreat from the world, make your home a quiet place on Sunday, and see if practicing a little bit of Sabbath doesn't help you find your own heart again. Try being instead of doing. You might like it.

Abundance is . . . giving yourself the gift of
time to nurture your spirit.

Come unto me, all ye that labour and are heavy laden,
and I will give you rest.

—MATTHEW 11:28 (KJV)

It does no good to think moralistically about how much time we waste.
Wasted time is usually good soul time.

—THOMAS MOORE

The trouble with the rat race is that even if you win, you're still a rat.

—LILY TOMLIN

God's altar stands from Sunday to Sunday,
and the seventh day is no more for religion than any other—it is for rest.
The whole seven are for religion, and one of them for rest, for instruction,
for social worship, for gaining strength for the other six.

—HENRY WARD BEECHER

Abundance is . . . an afternoon together with friends and family.

There is nothing like staying home for real comfort.

—JANE AUSTEN

Abundance is . . . Grandmother's silver tea service.

Abundance is . . . a crowded house, just for a few days.

*When senseless hatred reigns on earth, and men hide their faces from one
another, then heaven is forced to hide its face.
But when love comes to rule on earth, and men reveal their faces to one
another, then the splendor of God will be revealed.*

—MARTIN BUBER

Advent is a time to prepare our hearts to receive. Are you prepared to receive the gift that God wants to bring you? There are many gifts to receive. There is the gift of your family. The gifts of life that are especially delightful at Christmas: The sound of songs and carols. The sight of an excited child learning about giving and receiving. The scent of evergreens. The taste of homemade cookies.

Take the time to still your heart to receive the quiet gifts of each day that you are often too busy to notice. Listen and look and prepare your heart in the morning to be open to what the day wants to give you. Let Christmas speak to the deepest part of your heart where memory, faith, and hope reside. Prepare ye the way of the Lord and He will appear, because you are watching for Him.

Abundance is . . . an Advent calendar with lots of tiny pictures to
uncover as the days go by.

Abundance is . . . milk and cookies left for Santa Claus.

One of the most beautiful church services of the year, the Festival of Lessons and Carols, is performed by the King's College Choir and broadcast from King's College Chapel in Cambridge, England. Churches around the world also have their own versions of this service. In 1918 the great tradition of the King's College service of nine brief lessons, with carols to illustrate the meaning of the lessons, was begun. This service has been broadcast on the radio every year since 1928 (except 1930).

Opening with the carol "Once in Royal David's City," the theme develops: God's loving purposes for us from creation to the Incarnation. The order begins in Genesis with the fall of Adam and God's promise to Abraham, and moves on through the prophecies of Isaiah to Luke's descriptions of the Annunciation, the birth of Jesus, and the shepherds' visit to the manger, as well as Matthew's account of the visit of the wise men and John's as he unfolds of the great mystery of the Incarnation.

A dramatic opening with an unaccompanied solo boy's voice swells into a mighty chorus of praise and worship. Five or six boys are ready to sing the solo, but until the conductor raises his hand, no one knows which boy will be chosen as soloist. And then the song breaks the stillness: "Once in royal David's city stood a lowly cattle shed, where a mother laid her baby in a manger for his bed . . ."

Beloved in Christ, be it this Christmas Eve our care and delight to prepare ourselves to hear again the message of the angels: in heart and mind to go even unto Bethlehem and see this thing which is come to pass, and with the shepherds and the wise men adore the Child lying in his Mother's arms.

—FROM THE BIDDING PRAYER, FESTIVAL OF LESSONS AND CAROLS

The custom of the Advent wreath originated in antiquity in the Germanic countries. First pagans lit candles and bonfires during the darkest month of the year, December (or Yule, as it was called then), as part of the folk celebration of the winter solstice. In the early sixteenth century during the days of the Reformation, Christians reinvented the pagan custom. They created a circle of light, with references to Christ as the Light of the World.

There are four Sundays in Advent and four candles in the Advent wreath. Each Sunday a candle is lit, until all four are lit on the final Sunday in Advent. The candles vary in color from culture to culture, but each has a special spiritual significance in the story of mankind's fall and redemption. The first three candles may be red or purple, the other candle may be white, pink, or golden. They are placed within a tabletop evergreen wreath, or sometimes suspended on a wheel from the ceiling. As each candle is lit, an appropriate Bible verse is read. There are many Advent resources available to help you create an Advent wreath for your family.

But in this season it is well to reassert that the hope of mankind rests in faith. As a man thinketh, so he is.
Nothing much happens unless you believe in it,
and believing there is hope for the world is a way to move toward it.

—GLADYS TABER

Abundance is . . . lighting the candles of the Advent wreath.

Abundance is . . . a crowded shopping mall.

It is not the weight of jewel or plate,
Or the fondle of silk or fur;
'Tis the spirit in which the gift is rich,
As the gifts of the Wise Ones were,
And we are not told whose gift was gold,
Or whose was the gift of myrrh.

—EDMUND VANCE COOKE

I know Christmas has been overcommercialized and that the spirit of Christmas is not about material things. I personally believe that Christmas decorations shouldn't appear until after Thanksgiving instead of being rammed down our throats before Halloween is even over. But I must admit, I love department stores and downtown and malls at Christmastime. And I believe they are a sign that speaks to the desire of our hearts and God's longing to fulfill that desire.

The world asks, How much does he give?
Christ asks, Why does he give?

—JOHN RALEIGH MOTT

I love the crowds and the decorated stores. There's an excitement in the air that is missing all the rest of the year. There are packages wrapped in silver and gold, tied with red and green ribbon. Garlands hang over the heads of shoppers and Christmas trees catch the eye. Santa is on his throne and little children hang on the arms of tired mothers, waiting to see a stranger in a red suit and have a photograph taken. Toy trains chug around tiny landscapes in special displays. The perfume counters are piled high with once-a-year gift boxes full of the scent and mystery of winter elixirs. Colorful sweaters and beautiful dresses of velvet, lace, and satin are displayed in the women's department. The crowds ride the escalators, up, up, past floor upon dazzling floor.

Even when I don't have much money, shopping can be an exercise in delight and possibility. "Oh, that would be the perfect gift for Elizabeth." "I wonder if Ellen would like that." "I'm sure Dad would like this book." "When my ship comes in, I'm going to wear a velvet dress like this to an awards show." I'm a dreamer, so though I've had many a year when shopping meant only looking because I could not afford very much, I have been able to still find pleasure even without buying. And now as I get older and have begun to desire more simplicity in my life, shopping has become even less about buying things and more about experiencing things. I'm an imaginative shopper—imagining riches that money cannot buy. And I am a sacramental shopper, seeing a picture of God's grace to me in the superabundance of the American Christmas marketplace. It's all a matter of perspective.

When you shop, shop with love. Love not only the ones you are shopping for, but love the entire experience. Love the fact that you have a free choice and can shop. Love the crowds, the noise, the tired feet. Love the difficult-to-buy-for person and the dilemma of what to get the man who has everything. Love the delight of finding the perfect gift and love the disappointment of not being able to afford the gift you'd like to buy. Love the fact that a season like this exists; that even with all its faults it is a once-a-year reminder that freedom and plenty exist, at least for some people on earth. Understand that love has its price—and that price is found in joining in the all-too-human experience of seeking in earth's beauties a shadow of eternity's fulfillment.

And when you get home from the crowded streets and take your shoes off your aching feet, remember that you have been standing on holy ground. No matter how secular, commercial, or obscenely materialistic it might seem, there is a hidden holiness in the Christmas-laden stores and the brightly wrapped, dearly bought packages. The hopes and dreams that will be wrapped up along with the shirts and ties and dolls and perfumes and blouses and gadgets are a sign of yearning for the perfect gift from the Perfect Giver.

> *It's not what you'd do with a million,*
> *If riches should e'er be your lot,*
> *But what are you doing at present,*
> *With the dollar and a quarter you've got?*

—AUTHOR UNKNOWN

He who receives his friends, and takes no personal care in preparing the
meal that is designed for them, is not deserving of friends.

—BRILLAT-SAVARIN

Christmas is a time for hospitality. It's a time to bring out your best: bake your favorite dishes, decorate the table, dress up, and open the door to greet friends and family, welcoming wanderers into the heart of the home. According to Benedictine tradition, the monastery doors are never closed, but always open to all who come seeking the peace of God, without distinction of belief or background.

In this sacred and secular season of celebration, we, too, open our doors to all who would enjoy our hospitality. Our families contain a diverse cast of characters, all with different lives and different needs. And the human family also is a diverse cast of characters. It is at Christmastime that we are most free to welcome the world and open our hearts to its motley diversity.

Take advantage of the special nature of Christmas hospitality. This, more than any other time of the year, offers an opportunity to welcome and embrace people we might not otherwise meet in our daily lives—to spend time with those whom we do not see during the rest of the year. Because of the universal nature of Christmas traditions and celebrations, we have a unique chance to reach out to one another despite our differences, practicing a true hospitality of the heart.

Ah friends, dear friends, as
years go on and heads get gray,
how fast the guests do go!
Touch hands, touch hands,
with those who stay.
Strong hands to weak,
old hands to young,
Around the Christmas board
touch hands.

—WILLIAM H. MURRAY

Be not forgetful to entertain strangers:
for thereby some have entertained angels unawares.

—HEBREWS 13:2 (KJV)

*If one be gracious and courteous to strangers
it shows you are a citizen of the world.*

—FRANCIS BACON

*All guests who present themselves are to be welcomed as Christ, for he him-
self will say: "I was a stranger and you welcomed me." Proper honor must
be shown to all, especially those who share our faith, and to pilgrims.*

—THE RULE OF SAINT BENEDICT

97

A Small Collection of Favorite
Family Cookie and Fudge Recipes

Here are some family favorites for Advent and Christmas baking. These are all "family tested" and have been an important part of my Christmases over the years.

BON BON COOKIES

1/2 cup soft butter

3/4 cup sifted confectioners' sugar

1 tablespoon vanilla

food coloring (if desired)

1 1/2 cups sifted flour

1/8 teaspoon salt

cream, if needed

ingredients to fill cookies, such as cherries, dates, nuts, chocolate pieces

Heat oven to 350°.

Mix butter, sugar, vanilla, and food coloring (optional). Blend in flour and salt well by hand. If dough is dry, add 1 to 2 tablespoons of cream. Wrap level tablespoons of dough around fillings. Bake 1 inch apart on an ungreased baking sheet for 12 to 15 minutes until set but not brown. Cool. Dip tops in icing. Decorate.

Option: For chocolate dough, add 1 square unsweetened chocolate (1 ounce), melted.

A childhood favorite. I especially loved decorating these cookies with many-colored icings.

WALNUT CRESCENTS

1/2 cup butter or margarine

1/2 cup shortening

1/3 cup sugar

2 teaspoons water

2 teaspoons vanilla

2 cups flour

1/2 cup walnuts, chopped

confectioners' sugar

Cream butter, shortening, and sugar. Add water and vanilla, then flour and nuts. Chill 3 to 4 hours. Form dough into long rolls 1/2 inch across. Cut into 3-inch lengths, and shape into crescents. Bake on an ungreased cookie sheet at 325° for 15 minutes. Do not let cookies get brown. Cool, then roll in confectioners' sugar.

Delicate and delicious.

FUDGY BITTERSWEET BROWNIES

3/4 cup all-purpose flour

1/4 teaspoon baking powder

1/2 teaspoon salt

1/2 cup butter or margarine

3 squares unsweetened chocolate

1 cup granulated sugar

1 teaspoon vanilla

2 large eggs

1/2 cup semisweet chocolate chips

Line the bottom and sides of a 9-x-13-inch baking pan with aluminum foil; grease foil. Mix flour, baking powder, and salt. Melt butter in saucepan; remove from heat. Add unsweetened chocolate, stirring until melted. Stir in sugar, vanilla, and eggs. Add the flour mixture and chocolate chips until just blended. Spread batter evenly in pan.

Bake on center rack of a 350° oven for 20 to 25 minutes until top is firm when lightly touched. Do not overbake. Cool in pan on cooling rack. Remove brownies from pan by lifting foil by ends onto cutting board. Frost with confectioners' sugar frosting, adding mint or peppermint and green or red food coloring, as desired.

These are always a family favorite. A rich, deep chocolate brownie.

CHOCOLATE SNOWBALLS

2 cups sifted flour

1 teaspoon baking powder

1/2 teaspoon salt

1/4 teaspoon baking soda

3/4 cup butter

3/4 cup brown sugar, firmly packed

2 squares unsweetened chocolate, melted

1 egg

1 teaspoon vanilla

1/4 cup milk

confectioners' sugar to roll cookies in

Combine flour, baking powder, salt, and baking soda; set aside. Cream butter and brown sugar together till light, then beat in melted chocolate, egg, vanilla, and milk. Sift in dry ingredients a little at a time till the dough is stiff. Chill overnight. Roll dough into marble-sized balls and place 2 inches apart on an ungreased cookie sheet.

Bake at 350° for 8 minutes or until the tops are cracked. Remove from oven, and roll in confectioners' sugar while hot. Cool, then roll in confectioners' sugar once more.

Powdery white sugar on the outside, brown chocolate on the inside. Delicious.

RUTH'S CHOCOLATE DROP COOKIES

2 squares unsweetened chocolate or 6 tablespoons cocoa
(Mom says you might want to add a little more chocolate)
1 cup shortening or margarine, melted
2 cups brown sugar
2 eggs
1/2 cup sweet milk
1/2 teaspoon baking soda
2 cups flour

Melt chocolate and add to melted shortening; add sugar, egg, and milk. Sift soda and flour together and add to mixture. Drop by spoonfuls onto greased cookie sheets; bake 12 to 15 minutes in a 375° to 400° oven. When cooled, frost with white confectioners' sugar icing.

CONFECTIONERS' SUGAR ICING

Mix 1 cup sifted confectioners' sugar, 2 tablespoons cream, 1 teaspoon vanilla. Add desired food coloring.

CHOCOLATE BUTTER COOKIES

1/2 cup sugar

3/4 cup butter (not margarine)

1 egg yolk

1 teaspoon almond extract

1 1/2 cups flour

1/4 cup unsweetened cocoa or 1 square unsweetened chocolate, melted

Cream sugar and butter together; add egg yolk and almond extract. Beat until light and fluffy. Add flour and cocoa/chocolate, mixing well. Shape rounded teaspoonfuls and place 1 inch apart on ungreased cookie sheet, or use cookie press. Bake 7 to 9 minutes in a 375° oven till set. Cool and decorate.

Butter, chocolate, and sugar—what can I say? They're good.

CHOCOLATE THUMBPRINT COOKIES

1/2 cup butter, softened, or shortening/butter mix (half and half)

1/2 cup sugar

1 egg yolk

1/2 teaspoon vanilla

1 square unsweetened chocolate, melted

1 cup sifted flour

1/2 teaspoon salt

sugar or chopped nuts to roll dough in

Mix butter, sugar, egg yolk, vanilla, and melted chocolate. Add flour and salt until well mixed. Chill dough overnight. Roll 1 teaspoon of dough into ball and roll in sugar or chopped nuts. Place on cookie sheet and press thumb into center of each ball, leaving an indentation.

Bake 10 to 12 minutes in a 350° oven. Fill centers with confectioners' sugar icing mixed with mint or peppermint and tinted with green or pink food coloring.

Another chocolate/mint flavor combo,
but lighter tasting than the Fudgy Bittersweet Brownies.
A childhood favorite.

SPRITZ

2 1/2 cups sifted flour
1/2 teaspoon baking powder
1/8 teaspoon salt
1 cup margarine (you can use butter, but it won't taste like *my* Spritz)
3/4 cup sugar
1 egg, unbeaten
1 teaspoon almond extract
decorations for cookies, e.g., cinnamon imperials

Sift together flour, baking powder, and salt three times (actually, even though the recipe calls for this, we just sift them once); set aside. Cream margarine and sugar together till fluffy. Add egg and almond flavoring. Blend in dry ingredients gradually. Use a cookie press to form cookies on baking sheet. Add decorations (the little cinnamon imperials are my favorite). Bake 7 to 10 minutes in a 400° oven. (We usually check the cookies at 5 minutes and take them out just before the bottom of the cookie browns.)

Spritz are absolutely my favorite Christmas cookies.
Christmas wouldn't be Christmas without these.

SPRENGLER

4 eggs, beaten until light and fluffy

1 tablespoon butter (the size of a walnut)

* 1 lb. confectioners' sugar, sifted

* 1 lb. flour, sifted 3 times

1 teaspoon baking powder

salt

anise seed

Beat eggs, add butter, then add dry ingredients. Roll, cut out, place on cookie sheet, and let stand overnight. Bake about 10 minutes in a 325° oven until light brown (or till just beginning to brown on the bottom of the cookie).

(There was no measure offered in the original recipe for the salt or anise seed. I recommend 1/8 teaspoon of salt and 1 tablespoon whole or powdered anise seed.)

* 1 pound equals 16 ounces, equals 2 cups dry weight

This is an old family recipe and has been made by at least three generations in our family. I've copied it as it has been passed down.

SCOTCH SHORTBREAD

1/2 pound butter (real butter—no substitutes will do)
1/2 cup plus 1 tablespoon confectioners' sugar
2 cups sifted flour
1 tablespoon cornstarch

Cream butter and gradually add sugar. When well mixed, gradually add flour and cornstarch. (This dough can be mixed with a fork or a spoon.) Pat out on floured board and cut into desired shapes (my mother cuts it into squares). Punch with fork. Bake 20 to 25 minutes in 300° to 325° oven until set and bottom of shortbread is just beginning to brown.

These are solid cookies, white and butter-flavored.
My mother makes these every Christmas.

ROYAL SCOTCH SHORTBREAD

1 1/2 cups sifted flour
1 1/2 cups confectioners' sugar
1 cup butter

Sift the flour and sugar together; cut in the butter until the mixture is crumbly. Work dough into a ball with hands and knead about 10 minutes. Pat dough into 1/4-inch-thick rectangle, 14 x 12 inches, on a large, greased cookie sheet. Cut into 2-inch diamonds or squares with a sharp knife. (From my experience, this dough melts and expands over the entire cookie sheet as it gets hot, so be careful.)

Bake in slow oven (300°) 45 minutes until firm and delicately golden. Recut cookies at marks while still warm from the oven, and cool on wire racks. Handle carefully because these cookies are brittle and delicate.

*These are golden, crisp cookies, especially rich
and slightly greasy—but very good.*

PEANUT BUTTER COOKIES

1/2 cup butter

1/2 cup peanut butter

1/2 cup white sugar

1/2 cup brown sugar, firmly packed

1 egg

1/2 teaspoon vanilla

1/2 teaspoon salt

1/2 teaspoon soda

1 cup flour

Cream butters and sugars together. Add all other ingredients and enough flour (1/2 cup) to make mixture stiff enough for drop cookies. Arrange by spoonfuls on greased baking sheet; press flat with floured spoon (or use the bottom of a glass) and mark with floured fork. Bake in moderate oven (350°) for 8 to 10 minutes.

Mom made these when we were growing up.

KATHY'S SUGAR COOKIES

1 cup butter or margarine

1 1/2 cups sugar

3 eggs

1 teaspoon vanilla

3 1/2 cups flour

2 teaspoons cream of tartar

1 teaspoon baking soda

1/2 teaspoon salt

Cream butter and sugar together; beat in eggs and vanilla. Add remaining ingredients. Chill several hours or overnight. Roll out and use cookie cutters to shape cookies. Bake at 350° for about 5 minutes. When cool, frost with confectioners' sugar icing and decorate.

I had a roommate in the 1970s who was a whiz in the kitchen.
Her recipe makes the best sugar cookies I've ever tasted.

ENGLISH ROCKS

1 cup butter or margarine, softened
1 1/2 cups light brown sugar, firmly packed
3 eggs
3 cups flour, sifted
1 teaspoon soda
1/2 teaspoon salt
2 teaspoons ground cinnamon
1/2 teaspoon ground cloves
1/2 teaspoon ground allspice
1/2 cup buttermilk
6 cups pecan halves
1/2 pound candied cherries
6 slices candied pineapple, diced
2 cups pitted dates, coarsely diced
wine or brandy (my mother uses Marsala cooking wine)

Cream butter and sugar until light. Beat in eggs. Add sifted dry ingredients and buttermilk, mixing well. Pour batter over nuts and fruits, and mix thoroughly. Drop from teaspoon onto baking sheets. Bake in moderate oven (325°) for 20 to 25 minutes. While warm, sprinkle them with wine or brandy.

My brother-in-law, Eddie, loves these cookies. (My dad likes them without nuts.) These cookies keep for a long time.

PFEFFERNUESSE

1 1/2 cups margarine	1 teaspoon cardamom
3 cups sugar	1 teaspoon nutmeg
1 cup white corn syrup	1 teaspoon cloves
1/3 cup sour milk	1 teaspoon mace
1 1/2 teaspoon cinnamon	1 teaspoon ginger
4 teaspoons baking powder	1/2 teaspoon oil of anise
1 teaspoon baking soda	6 to 7 cups flour

Cream margarine and sugar; add syrup, sour milk, and oil of anise. Sift dry ingredients, including spices, together. Add half the flour to milk mixture until well mixed, and add the rest of the flour by kneading in. Chill dough overnight or longer, allowing the dough to season and the spices to blend.

Roll dough into thin ropes and slice with knife dipped in flour or cold water. Pieces should be the size of a hazelnut. Place pieces separately on greased baking sheet. Bake 7 to 10 minutes in 350° to 375° oven till golden brown.

Mom cuts this recipe in half because it makes so many cookies. These cookies keep for months. A handful is always a spicy delight to crunch on.

PAULINE'S MOLASSES COOKIES

3/4 cup butter, melted

1 cup sugar

1/4 cup molasses

1 egg, slightly beaten

2 cups flour

2 teaspoons baking soda

1/2 teaspoon salt

1/2 teaspoon cloves

1/2 teaspoon ginger

1 tablespoon cinnamon

optional: sugar in small bowl to roll cookies in

Combine butter, sugar, molasses, and egg; beat well. Combine all remaining ingredients; add to molasses mixture, mixing well. Dough will be stiff. Chill 30 to 45 minutes. Roll into 1-inch balls, then roll in sugar, if desired. Place 2 inches apart on greased baking sheet. Bake 8 to 10 minutes in 325° to 350° oven.

A family recipe from one of my songwriting buddies here in Nashville, Debi Champion. The recipe is from her grandmother, Pauline O'Bryant.

PAULINE'S SUGAR COOKIES

1 stick butter
1 cup sugar
2 eggs
1 tablespoon cold water
1 1/2 teaspoons vanilla
2 1/2 cups flour
1/2 teaspoon baking soda
optional: nuts or butterscotch morsels

Cream together butter and sugar; add eggs, water, and vanilla. Add dry ingredients, mixing well. Add nuts and/or butterscotch morsels if desired. Drop by teaspoonfuls onto greased baking sheet. Bake 7 to 12 minutes in 350° oven until the cookie begins to brown on the bottom.

This recipe is also from Debi's grandmother.
These cookies are delicate and buttery.
Debi makes them with butterscotch morsels.

SECRETS

1 cup butter or margarine

1 teaspoon vanilla

1 teaspoon almond extract

1/2 cup confectioners' sugar

1 teaspoon water

2 cups sifted flour

1 cup nuts, finely chopped (optional)

Blend butter, vanilla, and almond extract. Add confectioners' sugar; cream until fluffy. Add water to creamed mixture. Stir in flour (and nuts, if desired) until well mixed. Shape dough into small balls and place on ungreased baking sheet. Bake for 10 to 12 minutes at 300°. When cooled, roll in confectioners' sugar.

Another songwriting friend, Shawn Cushen,
offered this Christmas classic from his family traditions.
This recipe is from his mother, Dot Newsom Cushen.

OSLO KRINGLE

Boil one cup of water.

Melt in one stick of margarine (or butter).

Dump in 1 cup flour and take off heat. Stir till it all sticks together in a
lump in the middle of the pot.

Mix in 4 eggs.

Spread on greased baking sheet 1/2 inch to 1/4 inch thick.

Bake at 400° for 35 minutes.

Frosting is powdered sugar with 2 to 3 tablespoons of milk and 1 teaspoon almond extract.

*When I worked at a department store in the seventies,
one of my fellow workers gave me this recipe. It's easy to make and very
good. I've used his original words to describe the process. The instructions
may not sound elegant, but they work.*

SOUR CREAM COFFEE CAKE

1 cup butter

2 cups sugar

2 eggs

1 cup sour cream

1/2 teaspoon vanilla

2 cups flour

1 teaspoon baking powder

1/4 teaspoon salt

Topping:

4 teaspoons sugar

1 teaspoon cinnamon

optional: 1 cup chopped pecans or other nuts

Cream butter with 2 cups sugar. One at a time, beat in the eggs. Fold in the sour cream and vanilla. Sift together flour, baking powder, and salt; blend into creamed mixture. Place batter in greased 9-x-13-inch cake pan. Combine 4 teaspoons sugar and cinnamon together (plus nuts, if desired) and sprinkle on top of batter. Bake at 350° for about 45 minutes until the cake tests done.

This is our Christmas morning coffee cake before we open presents.
Mom makes it the night before.

CHRISTMAS FUDGE

4 1/2 cups sugar

1 can evaporated milk

1/3 pound real butter (no substitutes)

3 (6-ounce) packages of semisweet chocolate chips

8 ounces marshmallow creme

1 tablespoon vanilla

optional: 1 1/2 cups walnuts, chopped

Bring sugar, milk, and butter to a boil in a large saucepan. Cook 8 minutes, stirring constantly. Remove from heat. Add chocolate chips, making sure they are thoroughly melted in, then add marshmallow creme, vanilla, and nuts. Mix well and allow to cool. Spread in a greased pan (my mother uses a cookie sheet with sides) and let sit for several hours. Cut into squares and store in airtight container.

The fudge to end all fudges. I've never tasted better, not even at the most expensive candy stores. Mom received this recipe via an office memo from Dad's job. It's dated 12-22-52, the year I was born. As far as I know, Mom has made this every Christmas since.

How can they say my life is not a success? Have I not for more than sixty years gotten enough to eat and escaped being eaten?

—LOGAN PEARSALL SMITH

Thank God for dirty dishes; they have a tale to tell.
While other folks go hungry, we're eating pretty well.
With home, and health, and happiness, we shouldn't want to fuss;
For by this stack of evidence, God's very good to us.

—AUTHOR UNKNOWN

Enough is as good as a feast.

—JOHN HEYWOOD

PART 3

CHRISTMAS: A TIME OF CELEBRATION

Christmas is here,
Merry old Christmas,
Gift-bearing, heart-touching,
Joy-bringing Christmas,
Day of grand memories,
King of the Year!

—WASHINGTON IRVING

God chose what is weak in the world to shame the strong,

God chose what is low and despised in the world, even things that are

not, to bring to nothing things that are, so that no human being

might boast in the presence of God.

—1 CORINTHIANS 1:27–29 (RSV)

David watched his sheep there. Ruth met Boaz there. Jacob's love, Rachel, is buried there. The history of Bethlehem is rich in images from the stories of the Bible. Its name means "House of Bread," and it is fitting that the One who called Himself the Bread of Life should be born there.

The area is situated on a low but steep ridge in the rocky hills south of Jerusalem. Surrounded by green fields and lush olive groves, Bethlehem is also known for a very fine wine made from the grapes that grow there. Six miles to the north is the golden city of Jerusalem. To the east is a harsh wilderness, with the Dead Sea just beyond. Because the town is on the main route between Jerusalem and Egypt, there has been a caravansary, or inn, there since the time of David.

Bethlehem was not considered an important town at the time of Christ's birth, just as its favorite son, David, was not considered important as the youngest son of Jesse. David was a mere shepherd boy. But David was eventually crowned king of Israel. Little, unimportant Bethlehem became the birthplace of the Messiah. Sometimes our lives are like Bethlehem—we have to learn to see the potential in a common, unimportant place and allow God to come and do a miraculous thing there.

❦ ❦ ❦

But you, O Bethlehem Eph'rathah, who are little to be among the clans of Judah, from you shall come forth for me one who is to be ruler in Israel, whose origin is from of old, from ancient days.

—MICAH 5:2 (RSV)

One small candle may light a thousand.

—WILLIAM BRADFORD

And it came to pass in those days, that there went out a decree from Caesar Augustus, that all the world should be taxed. (And this taxing was first made when Cyrenius was governor of Syria.) And all went to be taxed, every one into his own city.

And Joseph also went up from Galilee, out of the city of Nazareth, into Judaea, unto the city of David, which is called Bethlehem; (because he was of the house and lineage of David:) to be taxed with Mary his espoused wife, being great with child.

And so it was, that, while they were there, the days were accomplished that she should be delivered. And she brought forth her firstborn son, and wrapped him in swaddling clothes, and laid him in a manger; because there was no room for them in the inn.

—LUKE 2:1–7 (KJV)

Abundance is . . . a tender lullaby.

Back over the black mystery of old years, forward into the black mystery of years to come, shines ever more confident the golden kindliness of Christmas.

—WINIFRED KIRKLAND

Christmas Eve offers a breathing space. The preparations are done. The presents have been bought and are wrapped. The stores are finally closed. Everyone who is going to be home for Christmas has safely arrived or is due to arrive soon. There is almost a catching of the breath, a sigh of relief, and a soft anticipation of what is yet to come.

On Christmas Eve many of us make our way to Christmas Eve services. A special dinner might be prepared. In my family, my brother-in-law, Eddie, is in charge of Christmas Eve dinner; he creates a collection of Middle Eastern specialties served with olives, bread, and his mother's recipe for Baba Ganoush. The tree is decorated that day, the presents placed underneath, waiting for tomorrow's opening ceremonies. Candles are lit. There are fresh flowers on the table. As the family gathers at the table, it is time to rest, find refreshment for soul and body, and remember a Christmas Eve two thousand years ago when a young couple gave birth to their firstborn son in a stable.

Some say that ever 'gainst that season comes
Wherin our Saviour's birth is celebrated,
The bird of dawning singeth all night long:
And then, they say, no spirit dare stir abroad,
The nights are wholesome, then no planets strike,
So hallow'd and so gracious is the time.

—WILLIAM SHAKESPEARE

The truth dazzles gradually
Or else the world would be blind.

—EMILY DICKINSON

And the Word became flesh and dwelt among us,
full of grace and truth.

—JOHN 1:14 (RSV)

The baby Jesus sleeps in a manger in Bethlehem, a seemingly ordinary child. The Bible says that God came to earth as a baby, grew up just as all children grow up, and became an adult. According to the Gospels, Jesus was not Superman, hiding His superpowers behind a Clark Kent mask, but one of us. Fully human and yet also mysteriously, fully God.

Whether you regard it as a primitive myth, literal fact, or mystical truth, the incarnation is the mystery at the center of Christmas. Scholars and theologians may debate doctrines and theories, but for me the Incarnation of Christ is a mystery to meditate on, a truth that offers meaning for the life I live today.

The Christian church has historically insisted on Christ as fully God and fully man. In a very special way the birth, life, death, and resurrection of Jesus Christ, His physical incarnation in time and space, is a sign to tell us who God is and how He relates to the world He created. I have meditated on this rich concept, turning it over and over in my mind like a many-faceted diamond is turned over and over in the hand, catching the light from one angle after another. The Incarnation tells me that our lives are important, affirming the Genesis "It is good" once again. It tells me that the body is not something to be ashamed of but to be honored. Place is important. We are all important as individuals and also as part of a greater whole. No place is too small, no person unimportant. Creation and God's presence in us offer a pattern of being that is so complex, beautiful, and wonderful that we can only understand a fraction of it.

There is a strong Christian conviction, substantiated by centuries of devout thinking and faithful living, that everything given to us in our bodies and in our world is the raw material for holiness.

—EUGENE PETERSON

The New Testament says that Christ is God come in the flesh. I love the way Eugene Peterson puts it in his modern translation of the New Testament, The Message. He says, "The Word became flesh and blood, and moved into the neighborhood." Christmas is about God coming to us, surprising us, showing up in unexpected places, right here in our mundane existence, in the midst of a life we often take for granted. Here He is, a helpless child, limiting Himself as we are limited, and even more important, joining us in our troubles.

The Incarnation, which is for popular Christianity synonymous with the historical birth and earthly life of Christ, is for the mystic not only this but also a perpetual Cosmic and personal process. It is an everlasting bringing forth, in the universe and also in the individual and ascending soul, of the divine and perfect Life, the pure character of God.

—EVELYN UNDERHILL

What good is it to me if Mary gave birth to the Son of God 1,400 years ago and I don't give birth to God's Son in my person and in my culture and my times?

—MEISTER ECKEHART

129

Christ came to a young couple who were not important in any scheme of the ruling elite of their day. He wasn't a far-off deity to be worshiped with fear and trembling in some golden temple. He was not an oriental potentate who ruled like a despot, demanding tribute and grinding us under the conqueror's boot heel. He was not a merchant prince, buying and selling our souls for a quick profit. He was just a tiny baby, born of a humble family, coming to join us in a troubled and chaotic world.

The highest service may be prepared for and done in the humblest surroundings. In silence, in waiting, in obscure, unnoticed offices, in years of uneventful, unrecorded duties, the Son of God grew and waxed strong.

—INSCRIPTION IN THE CHAPEL OF STANFORD UNIVERSITY

Men overlooked a baby's birth
When love unnoticed came to earth;
And later, seeking in the skies,
Passed by a man in workman's guise.
Only children paused to stare
While God Incarnate made a chair.

—MARY TATLOW

There was no political power, financial power, or religious power that had any interest or knowledge in the birth. Herod, that wily old fox of a king, only wanted to stamp out any possible threat to his throne, so his response to the wise men's news was one of violence. The temple priests had no interest and made no journey to Bethlehem. No, the only ones who came and worshiped were a few outsiders, wise men from another country, and a few scruffy shepherds.

Why would God hang out with a bunch of shepherds in Bethlehem when He could appear in glory in Jerusalem's temple just over the hill? Why would God come to a powerless family that had to travel to Bethlehem because Caesar wanted to make sure he got his full quota of taxes from a conquered people, instead of having the good sense to be born in a palace as a son of the ruling class, where at least He could have some political leverage? All through the New Testament, this God in Christ surprises us with whom He chose to hang around—sinners, tax collectors, and women of low repute. Do we get the hint that God likes us, even when our names don't appear on the social register? Do we understand that God says we are important, even though the world might write us off as total losers?

We have this treasure in earthen vessels.

—2 CORINTHIANS 4:7 (KJV)

When you celebrate Christmas, think about the importance God places on your life, even if you don't feel that who you are or what you do makes much difference in a busy world. The Incarnation tells us that we are special and unique and that God wants to dwell in our hearts. In God's eyes, there is no place too humble, no corner of the world that is not worthy to dwell in. He comes as a child to our hearts, not demanding or conquering. He comes as a baby to hold in our arms. It is not whether or not He is here with us. It is whether or not we decide to welcome Him into our lives.

Help me, Lord, to remember that religion is not to be confined to the church, or closet, nor exercised only in prayer and meditation, but that everywhere I am in Thy presence.

—SUSANNAH WESLEY

There is nothing so secular that it cannot be sacred, and that is one of the deepest messages of the Incarnation.

—MADELEINE L'ENGLE

Because of creation and even more because of incarnation, there is nothing profane for those who know how to see.

—TEILHARD DE CHARDIN

132

When love first tasted the lips
of being human,
It started singing.

—RUMI

Throw wide open your senses, longing intensely
with each of them for all which is God.

—HADEWIJCH OF ANTWERP, TWELFTH-CENTURY BEGUINE

Abundance is . . . red and pink and creamy white poinsettias.

The body is a sacred garment. It is the first and last garment;
it is what you enter life in, and what you depart life with,
and should be treated with honor.

—MARTHA GRAHAM

I say more: the just man justices;
Keeps grace: that keeps all his goings graces;
Acts in God's eyes what in God's eye he is—Christ.

—GERARD MANLEY HOPKINS

And he took a child, and put him in the midst of them; and taking
him in his arms, he said to them, "Whoever receives one such child in
my name receives me; and whoever receives me,
receives not me but him who sent me."

—MARK 9:36–37 (RSV)

No child was ever meant to be ordinary.

—ANNIE DILLARD

The gospel of love, creativity, and hope come together in the announce-
ment: "For unto us a child is born." All forms of love ripen and prove
themselves genuine by their fruitfulness in giving birth to something.

—SAM KEEN

If a man settles in a certain place and does not bring forth the fruit of that place, the place itself casts him out.

—SAYING OF THE DESERT FATHERS

Let us become the change we seek in the world.

—GANDHI

For mercy has a human heart;
Pity a human face,
And Love, the human form divine,
And Peace, the human dress.

And all must love the human form,
In heathen, Turk, or Jew,
Where Mercy, Love, and Pity dwell
The God is dwelling too.

—WILLIAM BLAKE

135

There is certainly something very touching about lambs, until they find
their way into holy pictures and become unpleasant.

—THOMAS MERTON

THE LAMB

Little lamb, who made thee?
Dost thou know who made thee,
Gave thee life and bade thee feed
By the stream and by the mead;
Gave thee clothing of delight,
Softest clothing, woolly, bright;
Gave thee such a tender voice,
Making all the vales rejoice?
    Little lamb, who made thee?
    Dost thou know who made thee?

Little lamb, I'll tell thee;
Little lamb, I'll tell thee.
He is called by thy name,
For He calls himself a Lamb;
He is meek and He is mild,
He became a little child.
I a child and thou a lamb,
We are called by His name.
    Little lamb, God bless thee!
    Little lamb, God bless thee!

—WILLIAM BLAKE

And there were in the same country shepherds abiding in the field, keeping watch over their flock by night. And, lo, the angel of the Lord came upon them, and the glory of the Lord shone round about them: and they were sore afraid. And the angel said unto them, Fear not: for, behold, I bring you good tidings of great joy, which shall be to all people. For unto you is born this day in the city of David a Saviour, which is Christ the Lord. And this shall be a sign unto you; Ye shall find the babe wrapped in swaddling clothes, lying in a manger. And suddenly there was with the angel a multitude of the heavenly host praising God, and saying, Glory to God in the highest, and on earth peace, good will toward men.

And it came to pass, as the angels were gone away from them into heaven, the shepherds said one to another, Let us now go even unto Bethlehem, and see this thing which is come to pass, which the Lord hath made known unto us. And they came with haste, and found Mary, and Joseph, and the babe lying in a manger.

—LUKE 2:8–16 (KJV)

I love the fact that it was the shepherds who saw the angels and came to worship the child in Mary's arms. Many of the shepherds might have been watching the flocks that belonged to the temple. The lambs they were shepherding were being raised to become temple sacrifices, and yet here in Bethlehem was also born the Lamb of God, as Jesus is called, who was to be the sacrifice for the whole world.

It's fun to speculate who the biblical characters might be if the event had happened in our day. I once heard a sermon that compared the shepherds to bikers, because that's the kind of image those shepherds might have had back then. Imagine a wild bunch of bikers coming into town on their motorcycles, kneeling in their black leather and studs to worship the baby born to a poor family visiting the big city all the way from a hick town in the middle of the country.

It wasn't the Wall Street millionaire in a Rolls-Royce, a platinum-selling rock star, a congressman, a famous TV preacher, or a glamorous movie star who found the Christ child in a stable. No, it was just a bunch of simple shepherds who saw a great light and heard the angels sing; who went to see the baby who would one day change the world. Just three wise men who came from another culture to find the King of the Jews.

And when they had seen it, they made known abroad the saying which was told them concerning this child. And all they that heard it wondered at those things which were told them by the shepherds.

—LUKE 2:17–18 (KJV)

Can you imagine what the neighbors thought? Think about what it would have felt like to have some wild-eyed shepherd tell you about angels and babies in mangers and the importance of an event that you, as a solid citizen of Bethlehem, had slept through. Oh, yes, you had noticed that there was a brighter star in the sky, perhaps. But you had been tired from a busy day of working at the shop, so a night visit from angels wasn't even a possibility you would entertain. Now here's a shepherd, someone from a social world different from yours, telling you that God has given the world a gift—and it's a poor couple's baby boy, out there in some stable. Yeah, right. Excuse me. Yawn. It's been a busy day, and I need to get to bed to get up early for work tomorrow. I think the shepherds have been out in the fields too long. Why don't they get a real job?

Would you have been curious enough to go see the child the shepherds were making all the fuss about? Would you have listened? Would you remember the strange shepherd's story thirty years later when a young evangelist was making waves in Judea?

> Abundance is . . . being in the right place at the
> right time for the right reasons.

> Abundance is . . . an unexpected gift.

ANGELS

Angels are never convenient visitors. They are always popping in at unexpected times and in unexpected places. They don't keep an orderly schedule. In fact, when an angel appears to a human being, the first thing the angel says is, "Don't be afraid."

I have never had a face-to-face encounter with an angel. But I have become convinced that I've encountered them, just the same. Sometimes it will be the angel of "coincidence," when events come together so beautifully that I could never have planned the perfection of timing and grace. Other times I have seen an angel work through a human being, rescuing me or pointing the way out of a situation. Sometimes I'm guided in my reading and find just what I need—or a friend offers a timely word that fits my situation perfectly, even though they knew little about my current struggle. Quite frankly, I think some angels guided me to certain quotes for certain sections of this book; serendipitous angels who delight in close encounters of the printed page kind.

Abundance is . . . an angel at the top of the Christmas tree.

Many people have stories of encounters with angels—there are books full of stories and even a popular television series. Whether you believe in amazing creatures with wings who break into our lives with big announcements or in hidden angels who affect our lives in unseen ways—listen. You might hear the brush of wings passing by or a distant music that is just beyond the reach of the human ear.

We not only live among men, but there are airy hosts,
blessed spectators, sympathetic lookers-on, that see and know and
appreciate our thoughts and feelings and acts.

—HENRY WARD BEECHER

The more materialistic science becomes, the more angels shall I paint: their
wings are my protest in favor of the immortality of the soul.

—E. C. BURNE-JONES

Abundance is . . . "every time you hear a bell ring,
an angel gets a pair of wings."

> And when eight days were accomplished for the circumcising of the child, his name was called JESUS, which was so named of the angel before he was conceived in the womb.
>
> —LUKE 2:21 (KJV)

People in the ancient world regarded names as highly important. The name for a child was chosen carefully and they believed that the name affected the child's character and future. When the Bible talks about "the name of God" and "believing in the name of Jesus" it does not mean an intellectual assent. In Hebrew this usage did not so much mean the name by which a person is called as it did his nature, so far as it was revealed and known.

Psalm 9:10 says, "Those who know thy name put their trust in thee" (RSV). This does not mean that the right word, *Yahweh*, is what the people trust; but it is the revealed nature of God, His character, on which they base their trust. Jesus' name, *Yeshua* in Hebrew, means "Savior." Another title that He is given is *Emmanuel*, which means "God with us." This reflects the essence of who He is—the One who comes not as judge and jury, but as Helper and Healer. He joins with us in our broken humanity and is not looking down on us in condemnation, but standing with us in love.

I believe that taking the Lord's name in vain is less about swearing and more about misrepresenting God and who He is. Using God's name or saying "Praise the Lord" as a thoughtless cliché is a way of tuning out the nature of God and turning Him into some automatic formula. Historically, people have abused Jesus' name by being more focused on getting the answers right and keeping to an often arbitrary standard than on Jesus' saving grace. As a result, sterile judgment of others came easily; loving them did not.

Our names are also precious. Our names reflect who we are—or at least that is what our parents hope when they give us the names we'll carry all our lives. Often we grow into our names or earn a new name when we have made an important life change. Language is a powerful force in our subconscious, and sometimes our names can grow us, as well. When I say the name of a friend or loved one, it does not matter that there may be a hundred other Roberts or Marcias in the world; when I say Robert or Marcia I think of the person, not their handle. And the person has made that name sacred because of the relationship we bear to one another.

A rose by any other name may smell as sweet, but I am inclined to agree with Anne of Green Gables when she said she believed a rose couldn't smell as sweet if it was called skunk cabbage.

When the name of Jesus was chosen for the child, it was given by an angel. And when the hymn writer wrote about Jesus being the sweetest name, it wasn't the fire-and-brimstone image of God he had in mind. Even if someone has taken the Lord's name in vain and used Jesus Christ as a weapon to manipulate people with, do not miss the true meaning of the name. Remember that it is the sweet fragrance of God's love speaking to you in a human language, not the condemnation or wrath of judgment. *Savior. God with us.*

> For thou didst form my inward parts,
> thou didst knit me together in my mother's womb.
> I praise thee, for thou art fearful and wonderful.
> Wonderful are thy works!
>
> —PSALM 139:13–14 (RSV)

As the print of the seal on the wax is the express image of the seal itself, so Christ is the express image—the perfect representation of God.

—SAINT AMBROSE

In the best sense of the word, Jesus was a radical . . .
His religion has been so long identified with conservatism—often with
conservatism of the obstinate and unyielding sort—that it is almost
startling for us sometimes to remember that all of the conservatism of his
own times was against him; that it was the young, free, restless, sanguine,
progressive part of the people who flocked to him.

—PHILLIPS BROOKS

Jesus came, not to hush the natural music of men's lives, nor to fill it with
storm and agitation, but to retune every silver chord in that "harp of a
thousand strings" and to make it echo with the harmonies of heaven.

—FREDERIC W. FARRAR

God had only one Son, and he was a missionary and a physician.

—DAVID LIVINGSTONE

When Christ came into my life, I came about like a well-handled ship.

—ROBERT LOUIS STEVENSON

To love anyone is nothing else than to wish that person good.

—SAINT THOMAS AQUINAS

For God sent not his Son into the world to condemn the world; but
that the world through him might be saved.

—JOHN 3:17 (KJV)

I think the greatest gift we can give anybody is the gift of our honest self.

—FRED ROGERS, TV HOST OF *MR. ROGER'S NEIGHBORHOOD*

One of the greatest gifts we can give at this busy season of the year is our time and our energy and our focus—the gift of ourselves. It's easy to fill our calendars and run from event to event. But I suggest that we trim back a few things in our schedules so we can take a little more time for each other. Here are some ideas for nurturing the gifts of love and friendship.

- Stop in for a cup of tea with a friend. You both need a moment to relax in each other's company and catch up.

- Take time to really look at the person you are talking to. Notice their eyes, their expressions, their mannerisms. Try to see this known and loved person as if through the eyes of a stranger or as if this were the last time you'd ever see them on earth. Notice the details that you normally miss.

- Talk less. Listen more. Listen with your heart. Concentrate on what someone is saying, not on what you want to say when they are finished talking.

- Do something to help a stranger with no expectation of something in return.

147

- Remember to show love through politeness. Saying "please," "thank you," and "you're welcome," are small, verbal gestures of honor for the sacredness of each human being. Helping someone with their coat or holding the door is a way of being aware of the other person's needs. Make sure you honor your family with these gestures, instead of only being polite to strangers and people you want to impress.

- Reactivate a relationship. You might want to call, or write a letter, or send a gift to someone you have not seen in a long time.

- Buy some wonderful stationery and write a letter to a select one or two friends. Yes, Christmas cards are nice. But isn't there at least one person who would enjoy a longer letter from you as well as a Christmas card?

- Stop holding grudges, criticizing others, and being resentful. These negative emotions steal your energy and your joy. Let go, forgive, and learn to move on, accepting that we are all imperfect.

- Choose a time to just *be* together with someone you love—without having to accomplish a goal, win an argument, or go somewhere. Light a fire in the fireplace, put some soothing music on, sip a hot cup of Christmas eggnog, and enjoy the moment.

*One of the most precious gifts we can offer is to be a
place of refuge, to be Sabbath for one another.*

—WAYNE MULLER

*We can make our minds so like still water that beings gather about us,
that they may see their own images, and so live for a moment with a
clearer, perhaps even a freer life, because of our quiet.*

—WILLIAM BUTLER YEATS

*Nobody sees a flower—really—it is so small it takes time—we haven't
time—and to see takes time, like to have a friend takes time.*

—GEORGIA O'KEEFFE

*Each friend represents a world in us, a world possibly not born until they
arrive, and it is only by this meeting that a new world is born.*

—ANAÏS NIN

This festival, which commemorates the announcement of the religion of peace and love, has been made the season for gathering together of family connections, and drawing closer again those band of kindred hearts, which the cares and pleasures . . . of the world are continually operating to cast loose: of calling back the children of a family, who have launched forth in life, and wandered widely asunder, once more to assemble about the paternal hearth . . . there to grow young and loving again among the endearing mementos of childhood.

—WASHINGTON IRVING

Abundance is . . . a fat, juicy roast turkey with all the trimmings.

Abundance is . . . home for the holidays.

Glad Christmas comes, and every hearth
Makes room to give him welcome now.

—JOHN CLARE

Eat what you like and let the food fight it out inside.

—MARK TWAIN

There is always room at the table for the unexpected guest, and I feel that the Christmas celebration, more than any other feast in the Christian year, is about including everyone. We are family, even when family includes strange Uncle Jim and dotty Auntie Myrna. Who else but family, of one sort or another, will embrace the cracked pots and broken vessels the rest of the world rejects as useless? In a world that likes people pigeonholed into neat categories, isn't it wonderful to celebrate a feast that welcomes all the ragtag members of this crazy quilt of a human family to a table set in honor of the One who claimed He was here to save the world in spite of itself?

Scruffy shepherds, wealthy Magi, seekers and believers, family and strangers—all are welcome at the Christmas table. And commercialism, though sometimes a rude guest, is allowed to bring a few presents to the party, as long as it keeps to its proper place. The reigning spirit is goodwill and peace toward all men and women and children (and animals). If God can choose to come to a stable, who are we to turn away His guests when they come to our tables?

So let us toast the season and welcome one another with warmth. Carve the roast, pass the mashed potatoes, and pour a glass of good cheer. It's the feast where winter's chill is forgotten in the glow of the family fellowship.

Our loving God wills that we eat, drink, and be merry.

—MARTIN LUTHER

All of us have experienced times in our lives that were so precious and special that if it were possible we would have had time stand still so we might live that moment forever. A good time is a taste of God.

—JOHN AURELIO

We say grace before our meals—not to make our food holy, but to acknowledge gratefully that it is already holy.

—WILLIAM MCNAMARA

The table was literally loaded with good cheer, and presented an epitome of country abundance, in this season of overflowing larders.

—WASHINGTON IRVING

Abundance is . . . gingerbread men and buttery spritz cookies.

Blessed be he who enters in the name of the LORD!
We bless you from the house of the LORD.

—PSALM 118:26 (RSV)

Peace and plenty for many a Christmas to come.

—IRISH TOAST

METHUSELAH

Methuselah ate what he found on his plate,
And never, as people do now,
Did he note the amount of the calorie count:
He ate it because it was chow.
He wasn't disturbed as at dinner he sat,
Devouring a roast or a pie,
To think it was lacking in granular fat
Or a couple of vitamins shy.
He cheerfully chewed each species of food,
Unmindful of troubles or fears
Lest his health might be hurt
By some fancy dessert;
And he lived over nine hundred years.

—AUTHOR UNKNOWN

Abundance is . . . Mom's special fudge recipe.

Abundance is . . . decorating Christmas cookies.

Abundance is . . . eating the cookie dough.

PART 4

PIPHANY: A REVELATION TO THE HEART

*The most beautiful emotion we can experience is the mystical. It is the
power of all true art and science.*

—ALBERT EINSTEIN

Wonder is the basis of worship.

—THOMAS CARLYLE

Again Jesus spoke to them, saying, "I am the light of the world;
he who follows me will not walk in darkness,
but will have the light of life."

—JOHN 8:12 (RSV)

God hides nothing. His very work from beginning is revelation—
a casting aside of veil after veil, a showing unto men of truth after
truth. On and on from fact divine he advances, until at length
in his son Jesus he unveils his very face.

—GEORGE MACDONALD

*E*piphania is the Greek word for "manifestation, unveiling, or revelation." Epiphany reveals that the child born in Bethlehem is the God and Ruler of the universe come to earth in human form. It also commemorates the visit of the three wise men, when they beheld the child they traveled so far to find. In the liturgy of the church this feast day also commemorates Christ's baptism in the river Jordan. It is also known as the Feast of Lights, celebrating the revelation of Christ as the Light of the World.

The Feast of Epiphany on January 6 is older than the Christmas Day feast and is the culmination of the Twelve Days of Christmas. Overlooked by the English-speaking world, Epiphany is called "Little Christmas" by the Eastern churches. Many countries save their gift giving and feasting for this day.

Epiphany is an important day for many Hispanic cultures. In Mexico it is called Reyes, or "All Kings Day." It begins with a symbolic reenactment of the visit of the three wise men and their offerings of gold, frankincense, and myrrh. On the night of January 5, the children put their best shoes under the tree, filled with hay to represent the manger in which Christ was laid. In some traditions it is the Magi who leave gifts for Epiphany morning and in other traditions it is La Befana, an old lady whose name is a corruption of the word epiphany. At night the rosca de Reyes, or "King's Cake" is shared. A tiny infant doll is baked inside the sweet, ring-shaped cake. The one whose slice contains the doll is considered king of the feast and chooses a queen. They will offer a dinner on February 2, Candlemas Day, when candles are lit in honor of the purification of the Virgin Mary. Another old tradition of Epiphany is the blessing of the house for the year. This is also the day when all the Christmas decorations come down in many households.

Epiphany is about the unveiling of God's purposes in our lives. So often we lose sight of what is real, and lose our souls in the daily grind. Or we think that we've got God all explained and in our pocket, that we understand all too well what should be done and what God isn't doing in our lives. But the Epiphany shows us that God comes in unexpected ways and in unexpected places. The wise men, or magi, were the first to see that Jesus Christ came not only to fulfill the Jewish prophecies, but also as a light to the Gentiles. We find our own epiphanies when we discover anew that God has a plan that is larger and wiser than our small ideas of what should be. Sometimes an epiphany moment will be revealed in the details of our lives; sometimes it is in the crises we encounter or unexpected journeys we have to make. God wants to make Himself known to us, if we will listen. He will shine a holy, radiant light on our darkness.

'Tis revelation satisfies all doubts,
Explains all mysteries except her own,
And so illuminates the path of life,
That fools discover it and stray no more.

—WILLIAM COWPER

Arise, shine; for your light has come,

and the glory of the LORD has risen upon you.

For behold, darkness shall cover the earth,

and thick darkness the peoples;

but the LORD will arise upon you,

and his glory will be seen upon you.

And nations shall come to your light,

and kings to the brightness of your rising.

—ISAIAH 60:1–3 (RSV)

Oh Christ, a light transcendant

Shines in thy countenance

And none can tell the sweetness

The beauty of thy grace.

In this may thy poor servants

Their joy eternal find;

Thou callest them, O rest them,

Thou lover of mankind.

—JOHN OF DAMASCUS

If, as Herod, we fill our lives with things, and again with things; if we consider ourselves so unimportant that we must fill every moment of our lives with action, when will we have the time to make the long, slow journey across the desert as did the Magi? Or sit and watch the stars as did the shepherds? Or brood over the coming of the child as did Mary? For each one of us, there is a desert to travel. A star to discover. And a being within ourselves to bring to life.

—AUTHOR UNKNOWN

Here is the part of the Christmas story that speaks most deeply to the journey of the heart. In the story of the wise men following the star, we see our own journey to find God, to discover the meaning in the pilgrimage of our lives.

Pilgrimage is an ancient image found in all religions throughout the history of mankind. We all are seekers after truth; we all long for a revelation. If we are wise, we will be searching the night sky for signs, aware that even if we have not yet seen it, there will one day be a signal that the divine is about to arrive in our midst. If we have great wisdom, we will even set out on a journey to seek the pearl of great price, to find our heart's desire. The long journey into the unknown will take us across deserts and abandoned places, through treacherous territory to face unknown dangers, to exotic climates and people with strange customs. Though we never leave home, the journey of the heart will still lead us in places we never dreamed of going, even into the valley of the shadow of death.

But there is light at the journey's end. There is a revelation to ponder, a word that is spoken, a sign that is given. It may be a cataclysmic life change or a new birth or a simple enlightenment, but God does answer the seeker's question. And in most cases, the answer is not what we expect—and often by the end of the journey we realize the question we were going to ask has been swallowed up by larger, more important mysteries.

Make room in your heart for questions, pilgrimages, mysteries, deserts, and stars. Find wisdom in the journey and know that one day, in this life or the next, you will come face-to-face with a God who loves you beyond all imagining.

When they saw the star, they rejoiced exceedingly with great joy;
and going into the house they saw the child with Mary his mother,
and they fell down and worshiped him.

—MATTHEW 2: 10–11 (RSV)

If seeds in the black earth can turn into such beautiful roses, what might not the heart of man become in its long journey toward the stars?

—G. K. CHESTERTON

THE STAR

Twinkle, twinkle, little star,
How I wonder what you are!
Up above the world so high,
Like a diamond in the sky.

When the blazing sun is set,
When the grass with dew is wet,
Then you show your little light,
Twinkle, twinkle, all the night.

Then the traveler in the dark,
Thanks you for your tiny spark;
He could not see which way to go
If you did not twinkle so.

In the dark blue sky you keep,
And often through my curtains peep,
For you never shut your eye
Till the sun is in the sky.

As your bright and shiny spark,
Lights the traveler in the dark,
Though I know not what you are,
Twinkle, twinkle, little star.

—JANE TAYLOR

To discover how to be human now is the reason we follow the star.

—W. H. AUDEN

Ideals are like stars; you will not succeed in touching them with your hands. But like the seafaring man on the desert of waters, you choose them as your guides, and following them you will reach your destiny.

—CARL SCHURZ

It takes solitude, under the stars, for us to be reminded of our eternal origin and our far destiny.

—ARCHIBALD RUTLEDGE

Some wandered in desert wastes, finding no way to a city to dwell in; hungry and thirsty, their soul fainted within them.

Then they cried to the LORD in their trouble, and he delivered them from their distress; he led them by a straight way, till they reached a city to dwell in. Let them thank the LORD for his steadfast love, for his wonderful works to the sons of men!

For he satisfies him who is thirsty, and the hungry he fills with good things.

—PSALM 107:4–9 (RSV)

There are but two classes of the wise;
the men who serve God because they have found him,
and the men who seek God because they have not found him.

—RICHARD CECIL

Then, opening their treasures, they offered him gifts,
gold and frankincense and myrrh.

—MATTHEW 2:11 (RSV)

There is much debate over who the three wise men were. Matthew's gospel calls them *Magi*, a word that refers to wise scholars, or possibly in old Persian a name for a priest of Zarathustra or Zoroaster. They were probably astrologers; later traditions called them kings, those men who came to find the King of kings. Legend names them as Balthasar, Melchior, and Caspar.

They came from the East, which could have been Persia, Iran, Arabia, or beyond. For them, the star signified the birth of a ruler. Imagine the surprise they must have felt when powerful King Herod knew nothing of the birth and when they came to find that the child they sought belonged to a poor family. Yet they knew when they arrived that they had reached their destination, and laid their treasures at the baby's feet.

The treasures the Magi brought are symbolic, foretelling the life of the baby. Gold represented kingship and glory, a symbol of Christ's role as the Son of God. Frankincense would have been used in the worship in the temple, a sign of His priesthood and messianic calling. Myrrh, which was used for healing and in preparing the dead, symbolized Christ's death and resurrection.

Brightest and best of the sons of the morning,
Dawn on our darkness and lend us thine aid;
Star of the east, the horizon adorning,
Guide where our infant redeemer is laid.

Cold on his cradle the dewdrops are shining,
Low lies his head with the beasts of the stall;
Angels adore him in slumber reclining,
Maker, and Monarch, and Savior of all.

Say, shall we yield him, in costly devotion,
Odors of Edom and offerings divine;
Gems of the mountain and pearls of the ocean,
Myrrh from the forest, or gold from the mine?

Vainly we offer each ample oblation,
Vainly with gifts would his favor secure;
Richer by far is the heart's adoration,
Dearer to God are the prayers of the poor.

—REGINALD HEBER

PART 5

THE SPIRIT OF THE NEW YEAR:
CELEBRATE THE ABUNDANCE

The nature of God is a circle whose center is everywhere
and whose circumference is nowhere.

—SAINT AUGUSTINE

Journeys, like artists, are born and not made . . . They flower
spontaneously out of the demands of our natures—and the best of them
lead us not only outwards in space but inwards as well.

—LAWRENCE DURRELL

Life is a journey. Christmas is a season to celebrate, but then life moves on. We go into the new year with resolutions to live a better life, to improve ourselves and make a difference. But sometimes the road gets long, we grow weary, and our good resolutions fall by the wayside. A life of faith is not built on our own strength, but on the strength and goodness of God.

I have become convinced that God is bigger than the boxes we try to keep Him in. And life is larger than the labels we would paste on it. God is big, life is large, and we, as Walt Whitman once said, "contain multitudes." We find surprises at every turn, unexpected mercy in times of need, and the love of God at the end of every road.

As you go into the new year, remember that the gift of Christmas is a gift for all times and all places. It is a sign that Emmanuel is with you wherever you go, whatever you do, no matter what. Give yourself grace and space to make mistakes—and do the same for others. We are imperfect beings, but we are also called to a greatness we can only faintly glimpse in our earthly lives. Be true to your dreams and encourage others to be true to their dreams, too. Respect the earth you travel on. And enjoy the journey.

Start small
Dream big
Live large
—JANA STANFIELD

One should hallow all that one does in one's natural life.
One eats in holiness, tastes of food in holiness,
and the table becomes an altar.
One works in holiness, and he raises up the sparks
which hide themselves in all tools.
One walks in holiness across the fields,
and the soft songs of all the herbs, which they voice to God,
enter into the song of our soul.
—MARTIN BUBER

The transformation required of us is not simply to be "like"
Christ, but to be a Christ.
—HILDEGARD OF BINGEN

You are hugged by the arms of the mystery of God.
—HILDEGARD OF BINGEN

169

Abundance is . . . a bustling airport full of Christmas travelers.

Abundance is . . . lost luggage found.

Here in this world He bids us come,
there in the next He shall bid us welcome.
—JOHN DONNE

Let not your heart be troubled: ye believe in God,
believe also in me. In my Father's house are many mansions:
if it were not so, I would have told you.
I go to prepare a place for you.
—JOHN 14:1–2 (KJV)

Winter is on my head but eternal spring is in my heart.
The nearer I approach the end, the plainer I hear around me the immor-
tal symphonies of the world to come. For half a century I have been writ-
ing my thoughts in prose and verse; but I feel that I have not said one-
thousandth part of what is in me. When I have gone down to the grave I
shall have ended my day's work; but another day will begin the next
morning. Life closes in the twilight but opens with the dawn.
—VICTOR HUGO

We are born for a higher destiny than that of earth; there is a realm where the rainbow never fades, where the stars will be spread before us like islands that slumber in the ocean, and where the beings that pass before us like shadows will stay in our presence forever.

—EDWARD BULWER-LYTTON

All around us we observe a pregnant creation. The difficult times of pain throughout the world are simply birth pangs. But it's not only around us; it's within us. The Spirit of God is arousing us within. We're also feeling the birth pangs. These sterile and barren bodies of ours are yearning for full deliverance. That is why waiting does not diminish us, any more than waiting diminishes a pregnant mother. We are enlarged in the waiting. We, of course, don't see what is enlarging us. But the longer we wait, the larger we become, and the more joyful our expectancy.

—ROMANS 8:19-25 *(THE MESSAGE)*

Prayer is our humble answer to the inconceivable surprise of living.

—ABRAHAM JOSHUA HESCHEL

After the celebration is over and we return to our daily lives, let us remember that we are no longer alone. God is with us. Emmanuel, the Prince of Peace, has come to tell us how much we are loved by the Father. Let prayer become a part of our day, a continuing conversation with a God who is interested in every detail of our lives. May the stories and traditions of Christmas help us keep the faith in difficult times, and may love be planted deep in our hearts.

Teach me, O God, not to torture myself,
not to make a martyr out of myself through stifling reflection,
but rather teach me to breathe deeply in faith.

—SØREN KIERKEGAARD

More things are wrought by prayer
Than this world dreams of.

—ALFRED, LORD TENNYSON

Stay with me, and then I shall begin to shine as you shine, so to shine as to be a light to others. The light, O Jesus, will be all from you. It will be you who shines through me upon others. Give light to them as well as to me; light them with me, through me. Make me preach you without preaching—not by words, but by my example and by the sympathetic influence, of what I do—by my visible resemblance to your saints, and the evident fullness of the love which my heart bears to yours.

—JOHN HENRY NEWMAN

*We miss the spirit of Christmas if we consider the incarnation as an indis-
tinct and doubtful, far-off event unrelated to our present problems. We
miss the purport of Christ's birth if we do not accept it as a living link
which joins us together in spirit as children of the ever-living and true
God. In love alone—the love of God and the love of man—will be found
the solution of all the ills which afflict the world today. Slowly, sometimes
painfully, but always with increasing purpose, emerges the great message of
Christianity: Only with wisdom comes joy, and with greatness comes love.*

—HARRY S. TRUMAN

$\mathcal{B}$ENEDICTION

The Lord bless you
and keep you
and make His face shine on you
and give you peace.
As you remember the Child born in Bethlehem
may you also remember to honor the child in your own heart.
May you follow the light of the stars in your dreams
and know that God is with you wherever you go.
Let the hope that was born in a stable
be a sign that God can change the world through one small child.
May the spirit of Christmas
warm our hearts all year long.
Grace and peace be with you
in the name of the Father and the Son and the Holy Spirit
as it was in the beginning, is now, and will ever be,
world without end.
Amen

I have collected quotes from many sources over the years, and many of the quotes in this book have come from my collection. Among the many other resources from which I have gathered quotes, I have found the following books to be the most helpful:

The Golden Treasury of the Familiar
Edited by Ralph L. Woods
© 1980 MacMillan Publishing Company

12,000 Religious Quotations
Edited by Frank S. Mead
© 1989 Baker Book House

The Treasure Chest
Compiled by Charles L. Wallis and Brian Culhane
© 1965 by Charles L. Wallis and © 1995 by HarperCollins Publishers

The Fairview Guide to Positive Quotations
Compiled by John Cook
© 1996 Fairview Press

Spiritual Literacy: Reading the Sacred in Everyday Life
Frederic and Mary Ann Brussat
© 1996 Simon & Schuster Inc.

I found an abundance of Christmas resources in magazines, books, recorded music, and Internet sites. And these are some of the books that were especially helpful:

The Frugal Gourmet Celebrates Christmas
Jeff Smith
© 1992 William Morrow and Company, Inc.

The Decorated Tree
Carol Endler Sterbenz, Nancy Johnson, and Gary Walther
© 1982 Harry N. Abrams, Inc.

A Continual Feast
Evelyn Birge Vitz
© 1985 Harper & Row Publishers

Christmas Spirit
George Grant and Gregory Wilbur
© 1999 Cumberland House

Christmas Customs and Traditions
Clement A. Miles
Reprint from a 1912 edition
Dover Publications, Inc.

Candy Paull is the author of the best-selling book *The Art of Abundance,* and she is a writer who has owned a freelance business for more than ten years, specializing in marketing materials for book publishers. She also has been a bookstore buyer and an advertising manager for a small publisher, for a total of twenty years' involvement in the publishing industry.

As well as being a writer and author, she is a published songwriter who makes her home in Nashville. Known for her encouraging lifestyle, Candy's philosophy of life springs from her experiences as a writer and musician involved in creative arts communities in Nashville and Seattle. She is available for speaking and singing engagements.

Candy Paull
P.O. Box 159276
Nashville, TN 37215

ACKNOWLEDGMENTS

Candy wishes to extend special thanks to Brandi Lewis, Victor Oliver, David Shepherd, Cindy Blades, Etta Wilson, and Nancy LeSourd for their help and encouragement. Without them this project would never have come to fruition.